Survival or *Revival*

Other Books by Carnegie Samuel Calian

Today's Pastor in Tomorrow's World (revised edition)

*The Significance of Eschatology
   in the Thoughts of Nicolas Berdyaev*

Berdyaev's Philosophy of Hope (revised edition)

Icon and Pulpit: The Protestant-Orthodox Encounter

*Grace, Guts and Good: How to Stay Christian
   in an Affluent Society*

The Gospel according to the Wall Street Journal

*For All Your Seasons: Biblical Directions
   through Life's Passages*

Where's the Passion for Excellence in the Church?

*Theology without Boundaries: Encounters
   of Eastern Orthodoxy and Western Tradition*

Survival or *Revival*
Ten Keys to Church Vitality

Carnegie Samuel Calian

Westminster John Knox Press
Louisville, Kentucky

Scripture quotations are from the New Revised Standard Version of the
Bible, copyright © 1989 by the Division of Christian Education of the National
Council of the Churches of Christ in the U.S.A., and are used by permission.

Book design by Sharon Adams
Cover design by Pam Poll

First edition
Published by Westminster John Knox Press
Louisville, Kentucky

This book is printed on acid-free paper that meets the American National
Standards Institute Z39.48 standard. ♾

PRINTED IN THE UNITED STATES OF AMERICA
99 00 01 02 03 04 05 06 07 — 10 9 8 7 6 5 4 3 2

Library of Congress Cataloging-in-Publication Data

Calian, Carnegie Samuel.
    Survival or revival : ten keys to church vitality /
Carnegie Samuel Calian.
        p.   cm.
    Includes bibliographical references and index.
    ISBN 0-664-25734-8
    1. Church renewal. I. Title.
BV600.2.C323 1998
262'.001'7—dc21   98-34781

In memory of

William S. Stoddard,

under whose pastoral leadership

I entered the ministry,

and

G. Albert Shoemaker,

whose Christian friendship exemplified

the people of God in action.

CONTENTS

ACKNOWLEDGMENTS

Every author is aware that producing a book is actually a team effort. My team includes my very able secretary, Linda Smith, who faithfully labored over various revisions of the manuscript. My wife, Doris Z. Calian, provided invaluable assistance throughout the production process. Hers is a significant voice from the pew in helping me to clarify my thoughts and expressions. Not to be overlooked is the wonderful staff at the Barbour Library of Pittsburgh Theological Seminary who assisted me in so many ways. My special thanks to assistant librarian Anita Johnson. My team also includes Charles DeMirjian, a committed layperson and a skilled wordsmith; during our conversations he made helpful suggestions that enhanced my sensitivity. My grateful thanks also to Mary Louise and Alfred Barbour who provided the perfect setting and respite to put the finishing touches on this book.

In this list of acknowledgments I wish to include the president and publisher of Westminster John Knox Press, Davis Perkins, who envisioned a book through an article of mine along with his colleague, executive editor Stephanie Egnotovich with whom I have worked directly. Stephanie has been gracious in giving me space and time in my busy schedule to complete this manuscript. I am indebted to her for her patience and support throughout the project. I want also to include my colleagues at Pittsburgh Theological Seminary for their stimulation directly and indirectly in my thinking, along with my students and countless pastors and parishioners with whom I have had contact through the years. An enormous thanks to all.

I have four audiences in mind for this book. First are the active church members who would like to see greater vitality and vision in their congregations of whatever size. I am hoping that these persons will form a nucleus in every congregation to study the book and implement the vision conveyed in these pages.

Acknowledgments

The second audience is the pastors who serve a pivotal role in leadership to bring about change and renewal in the life of the congregation. It is a tough and risk-filled task to take a church that is dreary and transform it into a vital congregation motivated by its vision to make a positive difference in the community. I am grateful to pastors who are willing to take on this challenge.

The third audience is seminarians who have the luxury to be both observers and participants in the process of renewal. It is my hope that this book will serve as a useful classroom text for them, as well as for church study groups. To this end I have included discussion questions at the end of each chapter to encourage dialogue among readers seeking keys to a successful church.

The fourth audience for the book is composed of the countless persons who seek a vital congregation to call their church home. Perhaps they will come to realize that in their shopping mall approach, they are part of the problem and part of the answer in helping the church to be the church. Therefore, I envision this book as a useful tool in membership classes in congregations and as a means of providing perspective for those seeking a church home.

I take full responsibility for all that is contained in these pages, with the hope that by God's grace this contribution might be a useful catalyst in your own faith journey.

Pentecost 1998
Pittsburgh, Pennsylvania

A Wake-up Call to the Church

Will churches merely survive or will they come alive in the twenty-first century? This is the real question facing most churches; the many publicized issues only cloud the picture. How do we work for congregational vitality as we enter the next century? What commitments are we willing to initiate and sustain toward this goal? Is there a singular vision for congregational vitality?

In this book I have identified ten keys to making congregations vital in the twenty-first century. First and foremost, congregational vitality calls for worship of God alone. This is easier said than practiced. Observers from Mars might have a difficult time sorting out the rationale behind many church services. Sometimes it seems the major portion of our services consists primarily of announcements rather than proclamation; more deference is sometimes shown to cultural allegiances than to God. At the center of congregational vitality must be an unapologetic worship of the triune God whom we confess to be our Creator, Redeemer, and Sustainer.

Second, congregational vitality calls us to be biblically literate. A congregation ignorant of scripture is a church without a divine vision. Biblical illiteracy makes a congregation vulnerable to cultural fads and numerous ideologies. The biblically literate worshipper knows that authentic worship is based on God alone.

Third, congregational vitality depends on understanding our history, its highpoints as well as its shortcomings. Knowing history well enables us to honor our heritage within perspective, avoiding the temptation of idolatry. As we learn to honor our heritage and its limitations, we will be in a better position to maintain our present identity without suffering from ecclesiastical amnesia.

Fourth, congregational vitality occurs when a church truly becomes a welcoming community. This implies an inclusive fellowship where the welcome sign is expressed not only in words, but also in deeds of hospitality. The diversity of our fellowship needs to be a sign of our strength and pride in one another. Wouldn't it be wonderful if following the worship service we not only had tea or coffee together, but actually took time to share a meal as well? We often become so comfortable with the "Sunday regulars" that we resent strangers, feeling they distract us from our sense of "community." A welcoming church cultivates a sensitivity to strangers and casual acquaintances rather than dismissing them with a brief smile and nod. Congregational vitality is characterized by the church that practices its own Good Samaritan's theology of caring concern and hospitality. Being a welcoming church is an effective and significant means of outreach.

Fifth, a vital congregation promotes prayer by establishing a network of prayer support groups. Prayer expresses our dependence upon the grace of God to empower us daily. A church that prays together not only stays together, but its members learn to become supportive of one another. Each prayer support group becomes a living reality of the church in action. A well functioning prayer group is never inactive and usually leads to community service. God's presence is felt and real to its members as we submit our wills and finite perspectives before the throne of grace.

Sixth, a vital congregation will pay attention to its youth. Nurturing youth sustains congregational vitality from generation to generation. Neglecting youth will undermine both our present and our future. We must seek far more creative avenues to reach our youth and be far better listeners. We need to address their questions, not offer leftover responses from yesterday's world. Nurturing the youth is absolutely essential for congregational vitality if we are to span the present generation gap in our churches.

Seventh, in every situation where there is conflict, a vital congregation will address issues with knowledge. We cannot allow rumor to dominate our thoughts and then act on incomplete data. How often do we react to perceptions rather than seeking the facts of a case when we are looking for worthy solutions to the issues that face us? In this information age, no one can be satisfied with minimal data. Congregational vitality depends upon and demands accurate information and honest, believable communication not only with members but also with the public.

Eighth, every time relationships break down and suspicion arises, we need to enter into a forgiving process, even though we cannot forget the wounds of yesterday. This is what Jesus taught and demonstrated. Congregational vitality depends upon becoming a community of the forgiving and the forgiven. Every church should be known in the neighborhood as a house of forgiveness.

Ninth, we need to work for peace and justice in our expanded neighborhood; through advanced technology we have become an international neighborhood. We cannot be indifferent to the unfairness and injustice done to neighbors across the street or to those on the roads of Bosnia, Rwanda, Mexico, and Northern Ireland. Congregational vitality requires attention to proclamation and to peace and justice issues as we carry out the biblical commission to reach out to the whole inhabited earth.

Tenth, for congregational vitality to become contagious, we must be people of trust. There is too much distrust in our midst today. We all know this. As we learn to trust God more boldly, however, we will begin to uncover the divine image in one another no matter how dormant or tarnished it may be. The first step in building trust requires faith—call it risk taking if you will—and it must begin with you and me stepping forward to initiate the process. Be prepared to be burned and hurt on occasion, yet have faith in the grace of God to uphold us through the landscape of brushfires surrounding us.

We have tall challenges before us if our churches are to be transformed into vital congregations. The choice is ours: Do we wish merely to survive or do we want to come alive in the twenty-first century? The wake-up call beckons.

Building a Visionary Church

God's Mission

*For God so loved the world that he gave his only
Son, so that everyone who believes in him may not
perish but may have eternal life.* —*John 3:16*

The Church's Mission

*We are called to be the people of God, the body of
Christ, worshipping, learning, and living out the
good news of John 3:16 within the world.*

Before we can adequately respond to the wake-up call we must
ask ourselves, do we truly desire to experience a new Pentecost
of vitality in our midst? We must be willing to have a change
of heart, abandoning, if necessary, old approaches and allow-
ing the Holy Spirit to guide us into uncharted waters. How else
can we become part of a visionary church? How else can we
enter the next millennium pulsating with new energy as the
body of Christ?

Welcoming a Willingness to Change

Building a visionary church is a major challenge facing all mainline denominations. What is needed first is an attitudinal
change, that is, a theological outlook that welcomes rather than
fears the future, that is willing to take risks when needed as the
Spirit pushes us beyond our limited horizons. The situation today is serious. For instance, since the time of my ordination in

the Presbyterian Church (U.S.A.) in 1958, I find the current numerical strength of my church reduced by almost one half, taking into account two mergers, with the United Presbyterian Church of North America and the Presbyterian Church in the U.S. It seems that the Presbyterian Church is becoming a skeleton of its former self while we continue to make excuses.

I believe that Presbyterians today are unfocused; our identity is unclear to ourselves and to outsiders. Confessionally we seem less committed to our heritage; denominational loyalty has eroded considerably. Presently we seem to be in a survival mode. This unhappy trend is also evident among other mainline denominations. It is urgent that we pay attention to strengthening our churches as institutions. Institution building ought to be a primary agenda item within the leadership circles of every church of whatever size. Any shared vision to unite church members that does not place an emphasis on institution building will not prove adequate. For everything we attempt to do through the church is dependent upon us agreeing that the church must continue as an institution in our midst.

In a 1995 symposium at McCormick Theological Seminary entitled, "Visions and Hopes for Parish Ministry," the Presbyterian moderator, Robert W. Bohl, reported that the parish church is endangered. He indicated that one-half to two-thirds of Presbyterian churches are struggling today to stay alive. There are approximately 11,500 congregations in the Presbyterian Church (U.S.A.); over eight thousand of these churches have fewer than two hundred members. What is going to happen, asked Moderator Bohl, when these small churches are faced with a five percent inflation factor added to their already modest budgets? His response: "They are going to die." Ironically, at the same time, Presbyterian churches are being urged to either start or add to their church endowments to confront this crisis of decline. If we work hard enough, we may become the highest endowed Protestant denomination, but still remain a remnant of our former self! More than money is required in the building up of a church. We seem to have overlooked the fact that the living endowment of every church is its membership, not the financial portfolios inherited from our forbears. Money is important, but it is not the principal building block on which to establish a visionary church. Ironically, endowments can actually reinforce churches' resistance to change as they cling to a dying status quo.

At the same time, according to Moderator Bohl, we seem to be witnessing "a theological Darwinism in our churches. It seems that those churches that are succeeding have little knowledge of those trying to survive." The ecumenical future of mainline denominations is in jeopardy; we are living in a time of crisis, and the window of opportunity for recovery is shrinking rapidly.

From my vantage point as a seminary president, I wonder whether the theological schools are interested or able to assist in this serious situation. Many seminaries are themselves facing difficult challenges and are preoccupied with their own survival. Seminaries also may be harboring guilt, believing they have exacerbated the crisis facing churches, and therefore tend to distance themselves from the grassroots struggle. Can theological education responsibly separate itself from these ecclesiastical battles for identity and direction?[1]

If theological educators choose to be engaged with our churches, they must be prepared for the impact of such involvement within their schools on program and curriculum offerings. We cannot afford to be unresponsive; the church expects a leadership role from theological educators. Furthermore, we cannot have visionary churches without instilling in seminarians a passionate vision of service.

I believe that theological schools can collaborate with the churches in a concerted effort to encourage an attitude for change with a visionary focus on faithfulness to God. As theological architects for the visionary church, we must continually ask ourselves if we have allowed sufficient space and time for the realities of change to be addressed. No ecclesiology is complete without a visionary spirit implemented within the organizational life of the church. We need to remind ourselves of the biblical admonition that, "Where there is no vision, the people [*of God*] perish." (Prov. 29:18, KJV).[2]

The Nature of a Vision

The heart of a vision is its power of anticipation—an anticipation that carries its own stamp of validity for the believer. The content of a biblical vision does not consist of wishes and unfulfilled daydreams. Abraham's vision of the promised land was divinely inspired, not an illusion; it was nurtured by signs and wonders during his earthly pilgrimage of faith. The apostle Peter's vision on the housetop sent him out to minister to Cornelius, moving beyond the Jewish community. Paul's vision on the Damascus road resulted in an expansion of the early church's missionary efforts.

A vision has within it a force that awakens our emotions and at the same time challenges the contours of our rationality. It is a spiritual view of what tomorrow can become that motivates and directs our ministry today. It is almost as if the Spirit of God is enabling us to enter into a virtual reality of the church, but without the benefit of advanced technology. We cannot punch out on the computer screen the exact dimensions of our vision; instead its dimensions are communicated to the inner recesses of our passion. Enlightened and empowered by the Spirit of God we are driven forward with a sense of urgency. We no longer are allowed to continue as usual; the Great Commission of our Lord once again has our attention. Building a visionary church starts then with fresh clues from God and is expanded through vigorous study of scripture and lessons learned from church history.

Establishing Core Values and Beliefs

With the above understanding, the first building block toward a visionary church is to establish our core values and beliefs. We need to prioritize what is absolutely primary and essential, and what should be secondary. We want a common ground of agreement on the primary values and beliefs that shape the church's culture. How well do we understand ourselves and the way we operate as a church? What is essential to the church's vitality and what needs to be pruned to allow new growth? How committed are we as followers to these essentials?

Establishing primary core values and beliefs depends on an organizational understanding of the church's purpose. What do we stand for and how are we viewed by outsiders? Some churches print their purpose statements boldly on their stationery. For example, one church claims: "To proclaim our faith in Jesus Christ and by the power of the Holy Spirit to love God and others as we love ourselves." Another reads, "Responding to the gospel of Jesus Christ—a ministry of discipleship." I would suggest, "God's forgiving love energizes us to serve." Behind these statements lies a theologically oriented core. Any church wishing to be visionary must be clear about mission and purpose. A purpose statement ought to sum up the visions that shape character and witness to the community at large. In short, the purpose statement communicates core values and beliefs strongly held by the congregation.

Genuine commitment to a chosen purpose brings credibility and integrity to the visionary church. These essentials are not negotiable and need to be remembered. The congregation must reaffirm its commitment regularly. Churches without vision are not clear about their core values and beliefs, and commitment diminishes when the going get tough. This is one major reason that causes confusion and an identity crisis. Without direction, how can any congregation make a difference in society? Theological educators can guide churches through diagnostic workshops to discern their identity, collective values, and beliefs.

An attitude for change is shaped by a church's primary core values and beliefs and by the active input of the congregation. The membership must be willing to take criticism, if need be, in defending and interpreting its mission to the neighborhood and beyond. The absence of strongly held convictions undermines individual loyalty to the local church as well as to the denomination. On the other hand, we are energized when we know what we believe and are willing to sacrifice for its preservation. This determination will be a sharp contrast to a social environment accustomed to endless compromises.

There is no place for compromise at the core of the church's mission. Yet compromising in a democratic society is expected and necessary. No one's action either in society or the church is above challenge. However, in our heart of hearts, we need to know what can or cannot be compromised if the integrity of the organization is to be upheld. When compromise is called for, do we know how to go about finding common ground for agreement? An organizational theology of the church needs consciously to follow a responsible process of negotiating through battles and differing interpretations. As we become skillful in such a process, we will advance as a community anchored to our basic tenets. Every conflict from the standpoint of an organizational theology needs to be seen from a historic perspective, reminding us that there are lessons to learn from the past. We must apply these lessons wisely to present conflicts, asking ourselves how this present issue will read in the future history of the church. Will this approaching battle look foolish in retrospect? Compromise is an integral part of public life for any community or organization; it is the process of getting along with one another.[2]

Once the faith community's values and beliefs are in place, they can serve as the necessary common ground for our identity and strength. This will enable the visionary church to face and survive controversy knowing that there exists a bonding communion in Christ. The community's unique character stems from a nonnegotiable attitude toward primary values and beliefs. At the same time, we must yield to the Holy Spirit, who continually leads and awakens us to God's surprising grace. This is what it means to be a reforming church able to discern between theological truths and ideologies; ideologies divert us from basic values and beliefs into a cul-de-sac in our journey of faith. Discipleship, in other words, has a twofold dimension: first, faithfulness to abiding convictions, and second, flexibility whenever the Spirit leads. The Spirit of God will give us the courage to seek new adventures, as did Abraham, Peter, and Paul. These adventures are not based on trendy styles or market surveys, but are Spirit led and involve commitment and personal cost.

It is always difficult within the church's organizational life to maintain a committed consensus, a common center of conviction and trust. Our failure at consensus building is undermining mainline denominations today. Unless we are clear and committed on core values and beliefs, our ecclesiastical structures are doomed to obscurity and obsolescence no matter how financially well endowed we are.

The visionary church with a clear sense of values and beliefs is much more than a fellowship of compatible people who enjoy one another's weekend company. Believers have a mission clearly distinct from service clubs and social agencies, as important as those organizations are. We are the people of the cross. As such we must prepare ourselves to bear the cost of discipleship. Unfortunately, the symbol of the cross has been eroded beyond recognition, so that the church today seeks to be everything to the community but the people of the cross. Many churches have even removed from their liturgy the forgiveness of sins and pardon, following the belief of some members that it might offend those who worship there! Without confessing our sins, how can we envision the kingdom of God? How can we sustain an urgency to practice the social and ethical implications in the Sermon on the Mount if we think so highly of ourselves?

This is why it is so important that every congregation be dissatisfied with the routine recitation and memorization of the Nicene and Apostles' Creeds. Every congregation must study and struggle with the roots of our heritage, as well as develop an ecumenical spirit of love and adventure. The organizational church has a never-ending task of reforming, articulating in today's language the creeds and confessions of yesterday.[3]

In each church we should be provided with the opportunity to discuss and formulate afresh what it means to be a Christian today. Our seminary classes and continuing education programs should be accessible to church members as well as clergy as we examine the basics that undergird us. The visionary church encourages every member to think through his or her confession of faith on a regular basis. Theological schools can also equip laity to assist actively in this process, empowering the people of God to actually be the people of God.

Embodying a Spirit of Openness with Reverence and Respect

In addition to commitment to a set of core values and beliefs, the second building block for a visionary church is to practice openness, especially in worship of God and respect for one another. Openness must be accompanied by humility in our quest for understanding the mysteries and tragedies of life. There are no easy answers in life; therefore we need to allow space for one another's spiritual journey, respecting the need for silence, for sermonizing, and for endless discussion and debate. There are many styles of spirituality welcome within a visionary church. We need to acquire skills to listen with greater empathy to sincere questions in the search for meaning.

A visionary church that practices openness will also become a laboratory of learning within a shared context of common values and beliefs. No one should feel intimidated; investigation of one's faith is encouraged within this safe environment. Nor should we feel offended if our views are vigorously critiqued. Our reverence for God and respect for one another should govern discourse within and beyond the community of faith.

Reverence for God will also humble us before the Eternal; we are unable to transcend our finiteness. Since we are created in God's image, our reverence for God also calls for our respect of one another. We are pledged to honor the reality of sacredness, we are all icons of the Divine.

Nobody within the community of faith should fear being reprimanded for not following a particular "orthodoxy" in vogue by the majority. Everyone's "orthodoxy" or "heresy" contains speculation as well as substance. The church as a nurturing institution of faith should provide ample room for self-expression in everyone's pilgrimage. We need to affirm one another's freedom to zig and zag in our journeys of faith. This is a significant part of our inheritance in Christ.

Hopefully, no one's ecclesiastical tradition will exclude the importance of ecumenical dialogue. A visionary church will foster intrafaith as well as interfaith dialogue, which should extend to agnostics and atheists as well. We must pull down barriers that exempt anyone from sincere dialogue. In the process, let us overcome fears and suspicions of unknown cultures; perhaps the Spirit of God is pushing us, like Peter and Cornelius, to new frontiers. All these efforts at dialogue warn us of the dangers of complacency and conformity, which can become oppressive conditions in any community of faith.

The visionary church characterized by this spirit of openness is also liberated from unhealthy dependencies on overbearing leaders who can be intolerant of other viewpoints in the community. No matter how high the level of integrity these charismatic leaders have, we need to be on our guard. Wise leadership in a visionary church recognizes the importance of everyone's ownership in the organization. In the visionary church, leaders are seen as followers and followers as leaders. It is from this vantage point that the people of God are empowered to serve. Together in a spirit of openness, we are called upon to build a visionary community of faith, nurturing wholeness within diversity to the glory of God.

John W. Gardner, former secretary of Health, Education and Welfare and founder of Common Cause, stresses the importance of maintaining openness for any visionary organization, especially in the context of today's diversity. Gardner is convinced that the day of the homogeneous community, with its emphasis on wholeness rather than diversity, is gone. He notes that homogeneity should not be preserved by practices we do not approve of.[4]

Gardner also indicates that "the nostalgic feeling of the old traditional community, which is of course in our minds the great seed bed of values, is hopelessly anachronistic. . . . You can't bring it back, and if you brought it back it would be hopelessly inappropriate. We have to be heterogeneous and have to live with the pluralistic." Gardner is particularly unhappy with the resistance to change so often found within traditional communities such as churches and theological institutions. Change is a reality of life. He worries that communities fail to move forward because of "the existence of long standing tradition." Community traditions are necessary he says, "but today you have to go out and create your traditions."[5]

"One thing is sure," continues Gardner, "the outward appearance of 'community' does not guarantee the inner spirit of communal effort." Gardner's studies of church congregations, for example, convinced him that there were "enormous differences in whether they were in fact 'communities.' Some of them have simply gained diversity, without discovering how to create a wholeness within which that diversity can live."[6]

Building a visionary church not only involves a dedication to core values and beliefs, but also a commitment to the process of openness to enable a diverse community of persons to experience wholeness for the mutual enrichment of all. Within this atmosphere of openness, the community can be more innovative than ever, reaching out with the message of divine love and forgiveness, not fearing change but welcoming it as part of its calling.

Maintaining Competency

The third block in building a visionary church requires maintaining the church's competency. This means asking: What is basic to the church's business and does the church fulfill this purpose well? Is the church clear on its primary purpose for existing? Have we been neglecting our competency, trying to be something we are not? An organizational theology invites the church to reconsider its behavior and practice. How faithful are we as a community of faith to our first and primary calling? "First things first," an often heard cliché, pushes us to remember priorities, but have we been diffusing our energies and talents in many directions and as a consequence neglecting our particular niche in society? This is to suggest not that we are limited to our niche, but that we should show prudence when we venture into areas not essential to our basic mission. Organizations often learn to regret the high cost of going far afield from their basic competency. How often has the church been amateurish in "prophetic" involvements in its intention to do good in society? Have we separated ourselves in these cases from our core competency? Every situation that beckons the church's involvement requires a judgment call that should be made through open discussion and mutual respect. An organizational theology promotes openness within the context of basic values and beliefs, mindful of our limitations and competency.

We can all be tempted away from our competency, becoming generalists in our zeal to help in every area without expertise in anything specific. As a result, we become engaged without doing our homework. Pastors, for instance, know a similar temptation when they spend time from their busy schedules reading everything but materials in their field. Admittedly, theological writings may take real effort to read at times. Nevertheless, the pastor, as the grassroots theologian to the community, is expected to keep up with information in the field. Unfortunately, theological and biblical materials are often viewed as irrelevant; pop psychology has become the main diet. As a consequence, some pastors are engaged in what I call "theological malpractice" without realizing their failure, similar to a medical doctor who neglects the expanding knowledge in a particular field or a lawyer who skips the research needed to help clients. Maintaining competency is the necessary balance to becoming well grounded. The organizational church needs to encourage as never before a learned discipleship, with deepening spiritual roots through study and prayerful fellowship. Only as we are equipped theologically and biblically can we make our ethical contribution in this changing world.

The competence of the church is primarily expressed through its nurturing function in worship, preaching, and teaching. This nurturing function flourishes as the members of a congregation become caregivers, mediators in justice and peace issues, and active participants in the community. The church as the people of God must respond to changing circumstances with much more than an either/or mentality. With keenly honed theological knowledge and pastoral skills, we are better able to solve problems within the church and the community. As the world shrinks and technology expands, consensus building within the church and the larger community will become increasingly more difficult. Being caregivers and peacemakers in the midst of these realities will not be easy. The visionary church must continually update knowledge and skills within its competency, thus bolstering efforts to enhance our society's quality of life in the name of Christ.

Toward the Visionary Church

Building a visionary church is an invitation then to all members to take ownership in the enterprise. A theological outlook for change is postulated on the premise that followership and leadership are interchangeable roles for clergy and laity. This is evident as we witness the increased number of tentmaking ministries (qualified clergy volunteers with other earning vocations) and certified lay preachers today, examples of role reversals among clergy and parishioners. A visionary church is a congregation liberated from unhealthy dependencies on charismatic leaders. A visionary church emphasizes being the people of God, a fellowship of imperfect members dedicated to pursuing God's will. A visionary pastor is committed to the spiritual growth of believers, not a series of self promotions. A visionary church sees the local organization of believers (of whatever size) as the body of Christ responsible for advancing the church's mission of nurturing, caregiving and peacemaking. The visionary church is never satisfied with past achievements; it strives to do better in giving its utmost to God. Finally, a visionary church continually works for wholeness among the members, exercising patience in digesting the diversity that healthy growth brings. Such a church is always seizing opportunities for service in the midst of changing circumstances.

The organizational theology of a visionary church is not a commitment to any single brand of theology as a path to the promised land. Most theologies have contributions to make and some even enjoy a period of limited dominance. Theologies have their seasons, but no single theological orientation prevails. A visionary church uses many theologies, understanding that all great pastors, preachers, and theologians eventually die. A visionary church looks beyond personalities, placing trust in God and building a unique culture and fellowship always open to the Holy Spirit. The efforts of a visionary church are directed toward building up the body of Christ, whose members are interdependent. The visionary church sees itself as a birthing fellowship, succeeding itself from generation to generation. The church constantly seeks to do the divine will until God's kingdom comes in its fullness. This ministry is never completed; the visionary church finds it incomprehensible when clergy sometimes say, "My ministry is finished here," and move on. This prevailing consumer mentality found in the pulpit and pew undermines community building in our churches. A visionary church places its present conflicts in perspective; it is always future oriented and encourages a spirit of innovation within the life of the whole membership.

What we need today more than ever are visionary churches driven by an organizational theology that places responsibility on the membership to be the people of God. To build a visionary church requires three essential building blocks. First, a set of core values and beliefs centered in Christ worth preserving and defending in the context of a reforming spirit must be identified. Second, there must exist openness that encourages creativity and discussion within the church and between the church and the surrounding society. Third, every effort must be directed toward maintaining the church's primary task. Organizationally, churches need to be aware of the harm they do when they drift away from their essential mission and competency. These then are the building blocks to a visionary church that can succeed in implementing the Great Commission set before us.

In this book, these building blocks are presented through ten chapters. Each chapter is like a spoke in a wheel, symbolizing our interrelatedness as we move together toward a common end. This wholistic or systems approach highlights that no aspect of the church's life exists in isolation from other areas of concern. The interdynamic relationships found within the church call for greater emphasis on team leadership among the people of God in the creation of a rejuvenated church singing again with enthusiasm as we enter the next millennium. Our discussion begins with the importance of worshipping God, who alone is the source behind all visions of redeeming value.

Worship God Alone

"You shall have no other gods before me" (Ex. 20:3). Worship services are those special occasions for us to renew and review our basic commitment to this biblical God who is displeased with all rivals competing for our devotion. We humans are natural worshipers; as a consequence, we always face the temptation of "falling in bed" with gods unworthy of our lasting embrace. When this happens we tend to be either too judgmental or too tolerant, while defending at the same time our freedom of curiosity as we sample one god after another from right to left and from left to right. After all, don't we belong to a generation of seekers, unwilling for the most part to make lasting commitments?

Barriers to Worship

Today's religious seekers it seems are interested in being short-term believers but not long-term joiners. This explains in part the growing tide of rootless spirituality in our society. It may also explain why we are no longer loyal to any single tradition. Various surveys inform us that over ninety percent of the population believes in "God," yet church attendance, especially among mainline Protestants, continues to shrink to an all-time low. Furthermore, the "God" that ninety percent believe in may be a far contrast to the biblical God. To examine with discernment which "God" deserves our trust is an undaunting task facing churches and theological schools in the next century.

Churches and seminaries dedicated to worshipping and interpreting the biblical God are committed to distinguishing their God from the false gods marketing themselves to us. Even so, many believers regard the task of naming the right God to be solely an autonomous and subjective pursuit of the individual without the aid of ecclesiastical institutions. As a result, we have increased public interest in spirituality and television angels and Hollywood films describing "God" to us, a description that may or may not correspond with the biblical God. These popular images of the supernatural further confuse us as we gather to praise the God of Abraham, Sarah, Mary, Joseph, and Jesus.

Worship services ought to be designed to usher us immediately into the presence of the biblical God who awaits our praise and wishes to address the anxieties and ambiguities found in our lives. Is this happening in today's worship experience? Is worship providing us the opportunity to have a divine encounter? Perhaps our praise and study of God are too closely associated with the cultural wars of our day, robbing us of an authentic worship experience. Is the use of latest media technology in worship an enhancement or a barrier to our desire to actualize God's presence before the congregation? Jim Taylor, writing in *Perspectives: A Journal of Reformed Thought,* humorously asks himself the question, "Is technology a blessing or a curse?"

> I started wondering what might happen if God got with modern technology and installed voice-mail. I imagined something like this:
>
> "Hello," says an angelic voice. "Thank you for calling heaven. We value your prayer and will make every effort to take care of your concerns promptly and efficiently. Please stay on the line; we can deal with your prayers more quickly than if you hang up and try again.
>
> "To help us direct your call to the party to whom you wish to speak please route your call as follows. If you wish to speak to one of the martyrs, press 1; to one of the saints, press 2; to one of the angels, press 3; to the Virgin Mary,

press 4; to Jesus, press 5; to the Holy Spirit, press 6; and if you wish to speak directly to God, press 7."

I pressed seven. I wanted to go right to the top.

Beep and beep again.

There was a long pause. The telephone line played a recording of Bruce Springsteen singing a Bach cantata accompanied by a choir comprising 2,000 clones of Linda Ronstadt. Then, a voice came on that was neither male nor female, neither loud nor soft. In fact, I couldn't even give it a quality—it seemed to vibrate through the very molecules of nature and permeate my cells and my thoughts. I knew it must, at last, be God.

"Thank you for calling," the voice said. "Your call is very important to me. I'm sorry, but I'm either away from my heavenly throne or tied up with another prayer request. If you wish to speak to my secretary, press 0. Otherwise, please leave a detailed message at the sound of the harp, and I'll get back to you as soon as I can."[1]

While many explanations have been given for the decline in church membership and attendance, my suspicion is that the church has become increasingly less relevant to its own members. This decline may also be due to boredom and intolerance with mediocre worship services that often cannot be distinguished from weekly service club meetings promoting good will and supporting business and professional interests. For others, the church has become simply a series of political caucuses where like-minded individuals seek to advance their favorite cause. Attend, for instance, one of our large church assemblies, and see the numerous advocacy booths on display. Some lose interest in the church when their cause no longer receives attention.

Many still go to church regularly, attracted to the inspiring musical performances and preaching. Professionalism in these high performance churches has turned congregations to audiences being entertained. Those attending, for the most part, know minimal commitment is demanded of the audience, which translates into token support. The other significant factor that draws many persons to church is the fellowship they enjoy among themselves, which at times is spoiled when strangers wish to join. Of course, there are exceptions to these generalizations, thank God! There are many joyful congregations with a visionary spirit that energizes everyone.

An Order of Worship

To move us in the direction of greater vitality and closeness to God, we may need to be more Quaker-like as we begin our worship hour. To start with, we could begin our services in silence, without music. There needs to be a quiet time for everyone, pastor and people, to settle down internally and to ask the Holy Spirit to transform our worship into an event of empowerment. In silence we have an opportunity to be more receptive to the Spirit's guidance, creating a sense of anticipation that our time together will be a blessing for us and for those leading us in worship. To assist us in meditating during our brief time of silence together, we might have an appropriate scripture verse or a poem printed in our bulletin focusing our attention and inviting God to create a spirit of anticipation within us.

Do not confuse this quiet time at the beginning of worship with the prelude. The prelude precedes the time of silence since many are still taking their seats. The period of silence begins when the organ stops playing. Save the "good mornings," announcements, and congregational concerns until the end of the service, after the blessing or benediction.

Following this period of silence, the liturgist calls the congregation together to worship God collectively. Together we praise this amazing God of grace whose love embodied in Christ is simply and elegantly symbolized by the cross and communion table. The hymns we sing inform us that we are sojourners, the community of God in the making; in worship we are seen as the people of God, the body of Christ.

All aspects of the order of worship should have this one principal task in mind: to honor and praise God who is our Creator, Redeemer, and Sustainer. The worship experience ought to empower us to affirm one another as God in Christ has affirmed us. The sermon offers an opportunity to articulate the gospel for our day, inviting us anew to commit heart, mind, and soul to God. Worship nurtures us into our responsibilities of discipleship before God. Ideally, as we depart from the worship service, we are left with a renewed dedication to the living God, and with enthusiasm we are called to undertake this day's challenges with joy, knowing we are not alone in this journey of faith and service.

Churches have spent too much time and energy discussing the pros and cons of traditional versus nontraditional worship services. I believe this is a misplaced conversation. The service should be centered on worshiping God, not trying to discern the acceptable level of entertainment expected by each generation. Instead, the service ought to be prepared to stimulate our imagination and sense of wonder, to lead us to a higher reality that liberates us from the excuses that imprison our spirits and prevent us from living with joy.

The order of worship should enable us to catch the spirit of transcendent reality; the human heart is hungry for those grace-filled moments that are gifts from God. I believe such experiences of grace are possible through numerous patterns of worship that defy easy labeling by us. In our order of worship, we need to provide spiritual space for one another, for the Spirit's creativity to work in our midst. If tomorrow's congregations become more intergenerational and diverse, no fixed categories of worship will be suitable. We need to work for a sense of order that provides room for experimentation.

As I noted earlier, the important time in the service set aside for announcements and congregational concerns should be separated from the proper order of worship. These comments should be printed and distributed to the congregation as they depart, with a few necessary items highlighted and announced after the benediction. A special prayer time for members who are ill and in special need should be held in a prayer service

19

before the worship hour on Sunday and during the week. I believe some arrangement of intimacy might be more welcomed by the congregation as we learn to respect the sacred hour for worshiping God, renewing and reviewing our lives before the Divine Presence, and praying and singing together for grace and direction for the week ahead.

It should be clear now why the church's mission is different from businesses and nonprofit organizations. The church's prevailing mission is to worship God; the seminary's prevailing mission is to study God and to worship God. Actually, on behalf of the church, the seminary serves two significant teaching roles. The first is in a custodial capacity to remind the faithful of their biblical roots and heritage; the second is to be a disciplined center of learning and research to enrich our faith and knowledge. The seminary's curriculum—theology, ethics, Bible, history, and pastoral care—helps us to avoid pastoral and theological malpractice in a litigious marketplace where the credibility of our faith is always being tested. This is why Jesus wisely shared with us the story of the Good Samaritan (Luke 10:29–37) with its examples of professional clergy who knew much about their religion but neglected its practice. On the highway of life they failed to live up to the test of authentic faith. The test of our convictions is seen in how we exercise belief and worship to make a difference in the marketplace. Ours is an incarnate God who demonstrated love and compassion to the people of Israel and at the cross of Christ. Can we afford to do less and be counted among God's faithful?

The God of Grace and Mystery

Worshiping God and serving others may not in themselves be enough to satisfy us in our journey of faith. We may in all candor still hunger for something more, as something deeper inside yearns for us to draw closer to God. What we desire and are often unable to articulate is a kind of mystical ecstasy or union with God wherein our personal tragedies are addressed and wherein our unanswered questions find answers. However, I am afraid most of us will continue to live with puzzling ambiguities and feelings of victimization because of our race, economic status, sexual orientation, age, experience living in broken homes, and from all sorts of tragedies. We will still be immersed in "cultural wars," which will come and go. Old enemies will be replaced by newer ones, and our moments of peace will be interrupted by conflict and loneliness. Nevertheless, we are called to move forward by the grace of God, encountering those modest and rare moments of divine ecstasy that join together the fragments of our lives into a seamless cloth covering our nakedness and vulnerability in a world that is electronically wired but disconnected in spirit.

We long for greater harmony and wholeness in our lives, but no church or theological education can promise that to anyone. With increasing disappointment, growing numbers in our society have opted for an uncommitted lifestyle, an open-endedness toward life. Since everything seems to be subject to change, they feel, why be engaged in any long-term commitments? And yet, to survive as human beings we need a coherent system of meaning at the center of our lives. If only God would give quick, bite-sized responses to our unanswered questions. Doesn't God know we live in a sound bite society? Our attention span isn't long; we yearn to close the gap between asking questions and finding answers. Sadly, many in our society perceive churches and seminaries to be sources of confusion rather than clarity for their lives. Responsible Christian education in our churches and seminaries should make us leery of any simplistic temptation that seeks to soothe our discontented spirits.

St. Augustine was right, there is a restlessness within us as we struggle to make our peace with God. But until we have reached this final union with God, we will continue to be tossed to and fro on a stormy sea with our faith, weak though it may be at times, as the only lifeline we have between us and any future with God. We will continue to struggle with our doubts, encouraged and thankful from time to time for those grace-filled moments of God's presence in our lives. The well-known writer Frederick Buechner confessed at a recent General Assembly of the Presbyterian Church (U.S.A.) that he was no longer a regular churchgoer. "I hate to say this," said Buechner, "but for many years now I've taken to going to church less and less, because I find so little there of what I hunger for . . . . It's a sense of the presence of God that I hunger for. It's grace that I hunger for."[2]

To me this deeper experience of worship, in which grace can be more frequently experienced, may call us to suspend judgment on the debatable agenda in our churches today, as we endeavor to more earnestly pray for God's grace to bring divine wisdom to our differences, and remind us once again that God is with us—Jesus lives! The Word of God is present among us. The Spirit of Christ is waiting for us to be still and listen.

Unfortunately, in our posturing with one another, many no longer seem to have the interest, passion, or energy to pursue this deeper relationship with God. The grace-filled moments elude us, those occasions when the conscious and the unconscious meet, transforming prayers for survival into prayers of praise and thanksgiving. In those fleeting seconds of divine ecstasy, words are not longer adequate, as our spirits are lifted by divine grace.

We can have those moments again if we honestly submit ourselves to do God's will, namely, to be cleansed, to forgive, and to be forgiven in our relationships with one another. The recovery of authentic relationships, divine and human, is the bottom line of God's agenda for the people of God. God is in the business of reconciliation. I suspect God is tired of hearing our prayers for survival. Instead, let us pray for a divine vision to free us from our addictions and self-imprisoning barriers. As Peter and Cornelius (Acts 10) prayed in their separate places, ghettoized by their wide cultural differences, each received a similar vision from God that dynamically transformed his outlook, enabling him to cross the psychic boundaries that divide and dehumanize. Their shared vision was indeed a grace-filled moment for Peter and Cornelius.

Finally, we need to realize that preaching, singing, and praying will not unveil the divine mystery to us. Neither will a traditional, nontraditional, or even a blended service do it. Nor will the pure study of theology reveal the divine essence to us. For that matter, the study of theology may lead us into greater ignorance and abstract propositions that are no more than mere speculations. The finite categories of human understanding can never capture God's being. We are engaged in a journey of faith, our convictions are woven with doubts. The few answers we have do not correspond neatly to every tragedy we face, nor will our "answers" stand up to empirical and rational measurements.

Yet we still hold on to our naked faith. Why? Because we trust in God. We believe that God is, we believe that God is with us in Jesus Christ, and we believe that this very God is also within us through the witness of the Holy Spirit. Through faith alone we approach this triune God who alone is deserving of our unconditional worship, whose divine presence defines our identity, whose encompassing reality gives us peace beyond understanding, and with whom we believe there is a glorious future.

The mystery of God is no longer a mystery to the communion of saints, for the dark night of the soul is behind them; their lives are now saturated in moments of ecstasy and union with God. This can be our destiny too. But there is no shortcut to get there. We need to be suspicious of worship experiences or theology courses that solve the mystery of God and answer most of our questions. Martin Luther and his reforming colleagues were clear on that score, for in the very revealedness of God in Christ they uncovered God's hiddenness as well. In other words, there is no Christology that resolves the mystery behind the life, death, and resurrection of the Incarnate One. What we have is the biblical testimony that we receive in faith as a reliable and authoritative witness to the God who reveals and hides at the same time.

As a community of God in the making, we should not undermine worship with attempts to name God in any limiting fashion, for any naming of the Divine will be less than accurate. Let God be God. The Incarnate One will also remain a mystery from a human point of view. Nor can we call God exclusively "he" or "she." Either approach makes God into an object, a being that is subject to our decoding. I hope that churches and seminaries in the future can overcome the gender politics of God fueled by the inflexibility of the English language. Any complete comprehension of God's true nature is beyond our grasp of full understanding.

In the final analysis, God is God. Whatever the limitations of language, we need to remind ourselves that God is neither feminine nor masculine, neither male nor female. As Margo Houts notes, "In the Genesis account, creation is neither *begotten* by a Divine body (male generation) nor *birthed* from a Divine body (female generation) but is, rather, spoken into existence by divine fiat. . . . The church has also consistently taught that the One who transcends gender nevertheless accommodates human limitations by using relational, gender-laden images for self disclosure."[3] The cultural milieu and language are significant factors in determining how believers speak of God. Language shapes our perceptions and anticipations. Therefore, all terminology representing God needs careful monitoring and balancing between statements of who God is (*positiva* theology) and who God is not (*negativa* theology) to avoid attributing to God inappropriate associations.[4] Houts illustrates that the suitability of language and methods depends on how the terms are used in any given context:

> Is God our Father? If by this the faith community means One who is powerful, nurturing, caring, faithful, transcendent Source, who speaks with authority and creatively (*via positiva*) and bears each of these traits to an eminent degree, without shortcoming (*via eminentiae*); if we do not mean that God is sexual, has male genitalia or masculine gender, is distant, aloof, absent, drunken, macho, or abusive (*via negativa*), then yes, God is our Father.

Is God also our Mother? If by this the faith community means One who is powerful, nurturing, caring, faithful, transcendent Source, who speaks with authority and creatively (*via positiva*) and bears each of these traits to an eminent degree, without shortcoming (*via eminentiae*); if we do not mean that God is sexual, has female genitalia or feminine gender, is enmeshed in and inextricably bound to creation, passive, dependent, or abusive (*via negativa*), then yes, God is also our Mother.[5]

Unfortunately, the Eastern Christian tradition of *via negativa* or apophatic theologizing has not been widely employed in the West. It could serve, I believe, as a useful ecumenical corrective upon Western theologizing. Apophatic theologizing tends to inform and humble us at the same time. We simply cannot know God's essence, only the divine actions that emanate from God and that are experienced by the believer as moments of grace. These occurrences of grace take us to the anteroom of the kingdom of God. This is why we are motivated to confess with unexplained joy that, "In life and in death, we belong to God . . . whom alone we worship and serve."[6] Furthermore, we confess, "Loving us still, God makes us heirs with Christ of the covenant. Like a mother who will not forsake her missing child, like a father who runs to welcome the prodigal home, God is faithful still."[7] Therefore, "With believers in every time and place, we rejoice that nothing in life or in death can separate us from the love of God in Christ Jesus our Lord."[8] This is also why the triune God is central to our worship, study, and life together as we discipline ourselves to be the faithful people of God, the body of Christ.

Discussion Starter

To worship God alone is at the heart of a visionary church; it is the essential foundation for congregational vitality. Discuss the "views of God" found in your congregation and neighborhood. Is there a consensus? Should there be?

Chapter Two

Be Biblically Literate

The Bible is big business in America. More copies of the Bible are sold in the United States than any other book; more versions of the Bible are published here than anywhere else on earth. Yet, in comparison to the number sold, it is one of the least read books. It seems, for whatever reason, that the majority of Americans feel it necessary to have a Bible as part of their household furnishings. For many, possessing a Bible is seen as an omen of good luck. For others, it is a useful item to have around; like a flashlight in a storm, you never know when there might be a need for it.

Owning a Bible, however, does not automatically make one scripturally literate! Unfortunately, this problem of biblical illiteracy is not only found in the pews, but also in the pulpits where often there exists little correlation between the pastor's sermon and the scripture lessons of the morning. Graduate theological schools cannot assume that seminarians possess a basic knowledge of scripture; consequently, a "Bible quiz" is required of students to test their rudimentary knowledge of the Bible. In turn, the experienced pastor cannot take for granted that congregations understand the different forms of the language of scripture, such as stories, metaphors, and images. Many scriptural references from the pulpit are foreign to most listeners in the pews. The situation is even worse among the millions of people who are illiterate, who lack adequate reading comprehension. At least twenty percent of the population in the United States is illiterate and hence biblically illiterate. As many as fifty percent of the chronically unemployed in our country are not functionally literate.[1] To those who cannot read well, the church faces a double task. Overseas missionaries among remote tribal groups teach natives to learn to read using the Bible as a basic text for instruction. Perhaps churches in the United States should also establish literacy workshops with the Bible as the means of instruction.

The Importance of Scripture

Why is knowledge of the Bible so important for building a visionary church and, in turn, congregational vitality? The answer is so basic that it almost escapes our attention: The Bible is the principal source for the information that contributes to our knowledge of God and knowledge of ourselves. As John Calvin emphasized, the Bible provides a framework that outlines our role and destiny. We believe the Bible is the most reliable guide to three significant questions that face us in life: (1) What may we know? (2) What ought we to do? (3) What may we hope for?[2]

We wrestle with these basic questions throughout our lives. As believers, we trust in God for the answers to these questions of ultimate concern, and scripture is the best source in shedding divine light on these questions. To be ignorant of God's will and wisdom is to suffer from spiritual poverty. Beyond a general lack of knowledge about the Bible, the sadder reality is that many sincere seekers are misinformed about and misuse scripture. Congregational vitality requires a scripturally informed church that can provide competent teaching on the significant questions of life.

Church members live in a culture that defines reality largely in terms of power, sex, wealth, and success. In fact, most of us know what we know from our struggles with these realities, and when we are troubled, we sometimes fantasize ourselves into this other world. Advertisers know this, and they appeal to our insecurities, inviting us to use their products and services to enable us to reach our goals. The biblical framework of reality is largely ignored as spiritual hunger mounts in society, as persons aimlessly seek a quick fix through pop psychology and pop theology.

There is no denying that we learn from personal experience and from the experiences of others. For instance, if we bite into a steaming hot pizza, we quickly nurse our mouth with a cool drink and we warn others to be careful. Our senses of touch, hearing, sight, smell, and taste inform us daily through experiences. A loving relationship informs us about love, and the experiences of anger and hate also shape our understanding of reality. Experience is certainly one way of learning available to humans.

Our knowing, however, extends beyond experience. We also receive knowledge by rational deduction or logic. Reasoning is another means of knowing that often paves the way for later reinforcement by empirical data. For example, Albert Einstein's formulation of relativity was at first a rational mathematical discovery that later was verified by experience. Rational deduction is another important means of knowing.

There is also an intuitive way of knowing, a hunch or a feeling that leads to discovery and knowledge. For instance, to what extent are psychic studies and detective investigations based upon intuitive insight? With many possible avenues to pursue, the detective and the scientist often focus intuitively on one or two areas leading to success. This way of knowing is subjective and more difficult to ascertain.

In contrast, the believer's way of knowing extends beyond experience, reasoning, and intuition. It involves disclosure by God; divine initiative is at the heart of the Christian way of knowing. This way of knowing is called revelation. We look to the Bible as the primary interpretive means of divine revelation. In fact, we believe the Bible is the most reliable instrument we have of God's revelation. This is why the Bible is authoritative for us. We believe that the Holy Spirit guides us through the pages of scripture.

Revelation is God's way of unveiling or informing us of knowledge that would otherwise be lost to us in our finite capacity. We shall never overcome our finiteness no matter how far we travel in space. God is simply infinite; the initiative to unfold divine mysteries does not belong to us. In our finite status there will always be a dimension of unknown mystery in our journey of faith. Beware of anyone who claims to unlock the secrets of God completely.

Revelation is God's way of unveiling divine purpose and meaning. The means of revelation are varied in scripture. For instance, Moses discovered the divine presence in a burning bush that was not consumed, and received the Ten Commandments on two stone tablets; manna came from heaven as a sign to the Israelites to continue their pursuit of God's will in the wilderness, and prophets foretold God's judgment upon the kings of Israel in their sins. Uppermost for Christian believers is the revelation of God in Jesus, the revealed Word of God made flesh. The advent of Jesus Christ reveals God's nature as forgiving love witnessed at the cross, bringing about the reconciliation of broken relationships (2 Cor. 5:18–19). What higher form of revelation from God can we ask for than this?

God's continuing revelation is centered in relationships. The Bible is actually the primary textbook on relationships, heralding the good news of reconciliation with God and with one another. Through relationships, divine and human, we are ushered daily into the realities of life. Reliable knowledge depends upon reliable relationships. In the Bible we have a standard by which the soundness of these relationships can be evaluated. Where healthy and renewing relationships exist, we help one another draw closer to God and understand more fully the meaning of life. On the other hand, unhealthy relationships leave us lonely and abandoned. No doubt this is why the French philosopher Jean Paul Sartre described hell as simply "other people." Sartre saw life as a series of broken and alienated relationships. How sad indeed!

The Issue of Interpretation

Scripture can be a tremendous resource as we engage in reflective dialogue with ourselves and others. God's word and way interpreted to us through scripture can serve to free us from external pressures, expand our horizon, and lead us to have hope instead of despair. But is scripture a reliable pointer to God? Is the Bible synonymous with God's revelation or simply an interpretation of that revelation? If it is the latter, how accurate is its interpretation? And which of our versions of scripture is more reliable than others? Even as we accept the significance and uniqueness of holy scripture as the initial interpretation of God's revelation, we still need to ascertain who are the most reliable interpreters among the scriptural experts who contradict one another's efforts.

In your personal study of the Bible bear in mind the following four suggestions that may prove helpful in clarifying questions as you read scripture: (1) Don't limit yourself to a single translation of the Bible. While I have chosen to quote the scripture passages mentioned in this book from the New Revised Standard Version, I do so for the sake of publishing convenience and the wide acceptance of this particular translation among churches. Actually, there are many other worthy and honored translations (for instance, the New International Version, The Message, the King James Version,) that will enrich your understanding of scripture, providing at times added insight on familiar verses. Develop a reference shelf of Bibles that are readily accessible to you, so that you can compare translations of any particular verse(s) under study. You will profit from a variety of Bible translations and may even wish to learn Hebrew and Greek to read earlier editions. Some laypersons even attend seminary for language instruction. (2) On your reference shelf, include some other valuable tools, such as a concordance, which serves as an index to words in the Bible and tells where to find them; a Bible dictionary to explain terms unfamiliar to you; and a Bible commentary, which can be one volume on the whole of scripture or a set of volumes. (3) Keep a journal or diary when you feel certain verses of scripture speak to your situation, and share them with others in a discussion or fellowship group. Exchanging thoughts with others will help you put your interpretation into perspective as well as provide new insights from others. (4) Read scripture in context. Examining isolated verses may not always reveal their true meaning. The use of a commentary often helps to place particular verses within a larger setting and thus reduces the chances for an arbitrary handling of a single verse or two. If you have access to a computer, you will find additional materials available to assist you in your personal study of scripture.

In addition to the above suggestions, we must always remember that we read scripture through the illuminating guidance of God's Spirit. This is why in my daily devotions, I normally utter a prayer to God to bless and inspire my reading and meditation of scripture. This is also why there is often a prayer of illumination before scripture is read in congregational worship. Calvin reminded us that "Scripture is the school of the Holy Spirit." This dependence upon God's Spirit in the reading of the Bible influences the dialogue between God and ourselves in our study of scripture. The Bible is the uniquely authoritative source to God's revelation and wisdom for us, yet at the same time, the Bible is not synonymous with God's revelation. For that matter, neither are our own interpretations to be equated with God's rendition. This awareness will keep us humble as students of scripture. Furthermore, the distance from the original divine revelation highlights the dangers and frustrations inherent in any attempt to be strictly literal in our approach to scripture. It also further emphasizes the need and importance of community sharing, since individual interpretations (and translations) of scripture may reflect solely the subjective needs of the individual interpreter rather than the message God has for us. Unchecked subjectivism in our interpretations is an ever present danger against which we must always be on guard. As we share scripture in community together, we will indeed discover that this divinely inspired book will serve us well as a "lamp to [our] feet and a light to [our] path" (Ps. 119:105).

The Question of Authority

With so many biblical translations and interpretations, individuals still may have doubts about the authority of particular biblical interpretations. Jews, Christians, and Muslims disagree over definite interpretations of Holy Scripture within their respective faiths. For Christians this struggle has been acute; the question of authority and authoritative interpretation of scripture continues to be a major barrier in the Christian dialogue among Protestants, Catholics, and Orthodox. From my viewpoint, the authority issue is the number one ecumenical problem among Christians of the past as well as the present.

Historically each Christian tradition (Orthodox, Catholic, and Protestant) took as its authoritative norm certain guidelines. These have been challenged in today's demythologized and deconstructive environment, contributing to what scholars refer as the "hermeneutics of suspicion." This interpretive attitude questions everything. Nevertheless, the traditional lines of authority still prevail. For instance, for the Orthodox, authority continues to be the ecumenical councils, the early church fathers and the wholeness of the church; for Roman Catholics, the papacy and its magisterium serve as the guardian over the heritage of faith; for Protestants, authority rests largely in the confessions and creeds begun in the sixteenth century and continued to the present. Each tradition has stressed the positive values of universality, antiquity, and consensus. Such values are in accord with the famous formula concerning authority by Vincent of Lerins in his *Commonitorium*, "*Quod semper, quod ubique et quod ab omnibus creditum est*" ("That which has been believed always, everywhere, and by everybody"). This formula, however, has not been entirely satisfactory, as evidenced in the ecumenical history of Christians. Today we must renew our trust in these traditional benchmarks of authoritative guidance in our respective traditions.

The issue of authority is integral to the interpretive process. The forms of authority are many—biblical scholars, councils, traditions, theologians, popes, to name a few. Each seeks to interpret the Christian heritage of revelation in an authoritative manner. Here two basic problems arise: the source of our authority and the transmission of authority. There is constant interaction between authority and interpretation; each generation seeks its own interpretation of the gospel and wishes to validate this interpretation by an acceptable authority. The lack of agreement on a single authoritative interpretation of scripture is a major source of anxiety and a dilemma for Christians. At the same time, church leaders (pastors as well as lay teachers) are not providing sufficiently informed guidance to church members. As a result we are misusing scripture today.

Ultimately, the quest for an authoritative interpretation of the gospel is a quest for God, "for there is no authority except from God" (Rom. 13:1). This search for final certitude is not possible for finite humans. Other than God, there is no ultimate authority; any pursuit without this recognition can only end in futile disappointment. To fill this need, various church traditions have emerged, promising authoritative interpretations for the hesitant pilgrim. Some young traditions have claimed to have received further revelations beyond the present canon of scripture. All these interpretations are under reexamination in today's ecumenical era, as Christian scholars strive to develop greater consensus among believers. Yet it seems any contribution from "experts" is seen as another human attempt to assert new dogmatism over earlier dogmas. In the end, Christians still lack a definitive and authoritative interpretation where there are no disagreements. In short, it seems that authorities are in search of The Authority.[3]

The search for an authoritative interpretation of scripture is ultimately a quest for God as revealed in the beloved Son, who

34

is the truth that frees and the power that saves. Neither external nor internal sources of authority will satisfy; only a divinely centered authority, the name of God as expressed on the lips of Jesus the Christ. Since the ability to be on an equal relationship with either God or Jesus is not possible, Protestants as well as other Christians are dependent upon the scriptural interpretation of revelation and the current activity of the Holy Spirit in the life of the church. Such dependence testifies that final certitude is not possible short of God. For many this is the time of waiting in faith; for others it is a time of frustration and doubt before proximate authorities.

Differing Views of the Bible

Because there is a wide range of interpretations of the biblical materials and no definitive authority acceptable to all Christian traditions, we find that those who possess a Bible can hold a wide range of views toward it. Let me briefly characterize seven contemporary views toward the Bible:

1. There are those who acknowledge the Bible as great literature, but are not really interested in establishing its authoritative status. In this view the reader is not required to regard the Bible as sacred scripture calling for some special allegiance. In college, I was encouraged to read the Bible as great literature in an English course, just as I would read Shakespeare. It was considered part of a good education to be acquainted with such literature, and of course lessons are learned from the reading.

2. There are committed believers who view the Bible as literal history. This position is in direction opposition to those who accept the Bible as great literature. Here the Bible is not only viewed as sacred history, but is accepted as literally authoritative on all subjects, beginning with creation and ending with God's judgment and the outcome for individual believers and nonbelievers. As literal history, the Bible is also seen as an authoritative guide in understanding such issues as economics

and science. There are, of course, more sophisticated nuances to this literal approach, but essentially scripture is accepted as literally synonymous with God's revelation—inspired, infallible, and inerrant. To budge from this stance is to enter a slippery slope of disbelief and diluted authority. Unfortunately, even literalists have differing interpretations of specific texts of scripture, resulting in far greater fragmentation within their fellowship than many publicly wish to acknowledge.

3. Some see the Bible as a collection of inspired stories with implicit moral lessons. Children's Bibles are often designed around these stories—baby Moses and Pharaoh's daughter, Samson and Delilah, King David and Bathsheba, the parables of Jesus. This is often a Sunday school view of the Bible remembered by many children and adults. Each story presents dramatic action and ends with a moral lesson. These stories have abiding value; however, they also have added implications beyond the simplified moral illustration.

4. Many adults view the Bible as an icon, a necessary and welcome item to possess in their homes as well as in their churches. The Bible's presence in the household serves as symbolic representation of God's presence in their home. It may be seen as a shield of protection. Within the civil religion of our society, the Bible is accepted as a cultural symbol; we see presidents and court witnesses sworn into position with their hand on the Bible. We dare to confess nationally that "in God we trust," and we illustrate that trust and presence by possessing a Bible. The Bible offers an iconic means of bonding, an accepted part of our ethos, and a cultural symbol within our society.

5. For countless believers the Bible is a personal devotional book. Their Bibles are full of underlined verses, which act as a "private Bible" within the Bible. Thomas Jefferson collected passages meaningful to him; his collection is known as the "Jefferson Bible." The remainder of the Bible was less significant to him. Those who underline passages in their Bibles often reread these portions of scripture regularly, but may be ignorant

about the rest of scripture. It is certainly good to have one's daily devotional time with scripture, but we should not equate this level of piety with being scripturally literate.

6. There are those, among them most seminarians and pastors, who view the Bible as redemptive history, that is, as the most meaningful interpretation of God's revelation. This is the most familiar understanding of scripture, as the student of scripture discovers, from Genesis to Revelation. In this view, the Bible recounts the unfolding of God's salvation history for humankind. A gracious God creates us and then witnesses our abuse of freedom, as we alienate ourselves from God and one another. From this perspective, the Bible is essentially seen as The Book on redemptive relationships, divine and human, illustrating through its content how God initiates reconciliation and expects us to also initiate a forgiving and loving process of reconciliation in our lives, thus uncovering the image of God in one another. The Bible as redemptive history is the dominant interpretation employed in most theological schools; in turn this viewpoint is communicated to parishioners through the preaching and teaching of seminary graduates. Together, pastors and parishioners are called upon to demonstrate through their lives that forgiveness and reconciliation are at the heart of what makes human life authentic and fulfilling.

7. Closely related to the redemptive view of scripture is the understanding of the Bible as the church's book. The church's early councils, guided by the Holy Spirit, defined the early canon of scripture—the sixty-six books that make up the two testaments of the Bible. (Some ecclesiastical traditions, such as Roman Catholic and Anglican, also include the books of the Apocrypha.) The totality of scripture is accredited to the church under the guidance of the Holy Spirit.[4] This is sometimes shocking for Protestants who believe that the Bible came before the church. Treating the Bible as canon and as a product of the church's early development makes us aware of

the historic realities involved in the interpretive process, namely, the subjectivity of the interpreter (I call it the *pre-text* attitudes) who exegetes (interprets) the *text* within the *context*. Differing contexts influence our interpretations of scripture. A balanced interpretation of the text seeks then to be fair to its original intent, while we sort the pre-text attitudes and varying contexts. This is why biblical literacy is necessary within the fellowship of the church, where competent leadership can provide space for parishioners to question, and where everyone studies together to understand and appropriate God's way and wisdom for our lives today.

This discussion closes with the insightful words of theologian William C. Placher, who views the Bible as simply a matter of trust. Placher wishes to replace a hermeneutics of suspicion with a "hermeneutics of trust."

> We trust the Bible because we have come to trust the God about whom it tells us. The process moves in a kind of circle: we also trust in that God in significant part because of what we learn in the Bible. Nor should Christians look, I think, for a single entry point into this circle. No one doctrine provides the foundation on which we believe all the others. We find ourselves trusting, in a way we sometimes find ourselves in love, without being able to define the steps that led to that state, and the elements that shape our trust are all tied together in complicated ways. Even a complete systematic theology will not fully explain such matters, but it follows that we cannot work out even a fairly good doctrine of Scripture without, for instance, a doctrine of the Holy Spirit and then, in turn, a doctrine, of the Triune God.[5]

Finally, Placher's admonition "to trust the Bible, to let it define our world and provide a language for thinking about the world, can transform our lives. But it does not make understanding the Bible easy."[6] The challenge is clear for us to be biblically literate in our churches if we are to experience a new Pentecost.

Discussion Starter

Becoming biblically literate not only enhances our trust in God, it provides us with a framework of what it means to be the people of God. So what is holding us back from being engaged in Bible study together? Is there only one right way to interpret scripture? If so, why? If not, why not?

Chapter Three

Honor Your Heritage

The Significance of Heritage

Why do so many church members seem not to know much about their own ecclesiastical history? Are they simply ignorant, or do they have selective amnesia, remembering heroic moments of their church's past and conveniently erasing moments of historical embarrassment? Whatever the case, we cannot live in a historical vacuum; we need roots and a sense of identity. And with identity comes the capacity to recall events and associations of earlier years, offering perspective in shaping our lives.

None of us can escape the importance of history. Whether we respect it or reject it, the good as well as the bad is woven into a tapestry that constitutes our past, individually and collectively. However, we seem to limit severely what we learn from our personal stories and collective history. This behavior among mainline church members expresses not only our growing disunity, but also reveals our ignorance of past battles in the church. We forget the lessons of the past. Or perhaps we selectively remember only what conveniently nurtures our biases? The teacher of Ecclesiastes reminds us how such practices will cause us to repeat our history and its shortcomings over and over again: "What has been is what will be, and what has been done is what will be done; there is nothing new under the sun" (Eccl. 1:9). Will we ever be able to break this chain of cyclical predictability? Will we find better ways to respond to change?

The disciplined study of church history offers us perspective and enables us to see effective and ineffective ways of responding to change. Change is inevitable for ourselves and for our churches. The forebears of our heritage were agents of change as well as victims of change. Their lives and thoughts have much to teach us.

God wisely commanded the Israelites, "Honor your father and your mother, so that your days may be long in the land that the Lord your God is giving you" (Ex. 20:12). Honor your parents, your founders; our existence is part of a larger human history. We did not simply come from nowhere; there is a biological history that makes you and me who we are. Likewise, there is a complex spiritual dynamic involved in the birthing of an ecclesiastical tradition. We may never know the whole story, but we are duty bound to acknowledge the journey our church has traveled as we encounter the forks and potholes in the road today. One's ecclesiastical heritage is a significant map to aid us in entering new pathways. For those without any church home past or present, knowing our heritage can provide them direction; it can also give them perspective in their long journey to find a spiritual home.

We are not called upon to idealize our founders nor to turn them into idols. Rather, we are called upon to honor our beginnings ("Honor your father and your mother"). No birthing process, human or ecclesiastical, is done in a vacuum. To honor our heritage is to gain an understanding of our beginning and, in retrospect, to develop appreciation for the present moment from the viewpoint of the past. The search for common ground on which to base denominational unity calls for the rediscovery of our history. We have discovered the importance of uncovering one's past in today's therapeutic society. Insights gained through authentic dialogue have a way of liberating us to accept ourselves, removing the guilt that sometimes paralyzes us. For many, the lessons learned have a way of energizing us to reach beyond the limitations of the past and experience divine grace anew. It also enables us to build positively on the foundation of God's image bequeathed to each of us.

No one's ecclesiastical heritage or personal history is without shortcomings. Nonetheless, when studied, this heritage becomes a vital force in reviving congregations to not only recognize their humanity, but also to experience the Spirit's efforts in their church's history. This is the vision glorious waiting to be reclaimed through a careful study of history. Honoring our heritage then is an underutilized source of vitality urging us toward greater heights in our journey of faith.

But wait a minute, some may urge. Aren't the issues different? And haven't the players changed? Why waste our energies on the past? Besides, aren't we entering a postdenominational era? True, there is a great deal of discussion on this among scholars and seminarians, but there is no conclusive determination as yet. Perhaps we have accepted this postdenominational designation uncritically. What is the evidence to date? Perhaps the church on a national level (for example, through the National Council of Churches) should contract with a research marketing firm to do for us what professionals do for the business community, namely, to provide a better understanding of our members and the potential constituency we wish to reach.[1] This might be research money well spent if we are willing to take the findings seriously in making future plans. Meanwhile, I am withholding judgment as to whether or not we are living in a postdenominational context, in spite of the mushrooming of nondenominational, independent megachurches (which have now formed their own associations).

Moreover, my focus (shared, I hope, by denominational churches) is to reach the homeless church constituency that has rapidly increased in recent decades. Cutting across generational lines, this group includes former church members and those who have probably never joined. Together they make up the largest proportion of spiritual drifters, shopping in a haphazard fashion for the "perfect congregation," which continues to elude them. For this group, whether a church is

43

denominationally related or independent is of secondary importance. They desire to be embraced by a supportive fellowship led by a "near perfect" pastor. It is beginning to dawn upon this homeless church crowd that there exists neither a perfect church nor a perfect pastor.

Frankly, I have yet to find any perfect seminarians either. We certainly have dedicated and competent candidates at our seminaries preparing for ministry, but none are without shortcomings. Nor can I imagine for the foreseeable future (based on my thirty-five years of teaching in theological settings) that the situation will change. We will continue to graduate imperfect seminarians to minister to imperfect congregations as imperfect pastors. There is no theological curriculum on earth that can produce perfection. So what can we do to reach the homeless church constituency of all ages and motivate them to make a commitment?

To begin with, denominational churches need to regain pride in their history. What made their heritage great? How can we implement the pioneering spirit of our forebears and learn from their errors? The appeal of today's denominational church needs to be based on more than a marketing analysis; we must recover the strengths of our respective traditions and rediscover the shared leadership that clergy and laity together enjoyed as the people of God. We are currently imbalanced, depending too much on clergy and not enough on the laity. This needs to be corrected.[2] I believe the independent megachurches are trying to remedy the neglected role of the laity. These megachurches blame this neglect on clericalism nurtured by seminaries, hence their wish to conduct their own educational programs as a corrective. Seminaries need to listen to what these churches are saying. Laypersons need to be more welcomed on seminary campuses. We must provide more programs and courses for laity in a conscious effort to build up the people of God. Honoring our heritage will point us toward the vision that motivated our forebears to reform the church in the face of change and corruption. Honoring our heritage provides lessons on how the church successfully and unsuccessfully maintained its creative tension between continuity and discontinuity in response to the future. An ignorance of church history will doom us to repeat our errors.

As we continue in our faith journey, no doubt our feelings toward the church will oscillate between frustration and faithfulness, but we must never lose sight of the biblical vision for outreach inspired by the teaching of John 3:16. The church of various traditions is still the best vehicle to pursue this outreach. Romanian author Petru Dumitriu has expressed well his own struggles with faith and his church:

> It is impossible to be a Christian.
> It is impossible not to be a Christian.
> It is impossible to be a Christian outside the Church,
> And the Church is impossible.[3]

The Sovereignty of God's Grace: The Reformed Story

There is a story behind everyone's search for a church home. I came to the Presbyterian Church by adoption; I was not born into a Presbyterian family. I joined the church during my sophomore year in college. I was drawn to the church's order of worship, the finely crafted sermons and prayers, the quality of music and choice of hymns, the accepting fellowship of peers, and the welcoming attitude in church classes that encouraged an inquisitive mind to ask questions as we sought together to establish a deeper faith commitment. In time, I discovered that most of these particular traits of the local Presbyterian Church were due in no small part to its historic tradition that nurtured theological reflection, inviting persons to be thinking as well as caring Christians.

Today, nearly sixty percent of members are new to the Presbyterian Church (U.S.A.). We Presbyterians belong to a larger family of churches referred to as Reformed. Our heritage is associated with the Swiss Reformers of the sixteenth century.

45

Two of these were Ulrich (Huldreich) Zwingli (1484–1531) of Zurich and John Calvin (1509–1564), who came to Geneva as an immigrant from France.[4] We continue to be influenced by Calvin's legacy of writings, especially his *Institutes of the Christian Religion.*

Presbyterians have long been identified as proponents of predestination, but a more significant characteristic is an emphasis on "always being reformed" according to the Word of God. The popular Latin phrase, "Ecclesia Reformata, semper reformanda" ("The church reformed and always being reformed") places importance on the church's need to seek constant renewal. The church is a living organism, subject to the leading of the Holy Spirit. Implicit in the Presbyterian understanding of the church is dissatisfaction with the status quo. The church is always in need of improvement; we must never stop learning with relevance and sensitivity in response to changing realities. At the heart of the Reformed tradition is an essential commitment to God's grace witnessed in scripture, encountered in Christ, and experienced in daily life.

Trusting in the sufficiency of God's grace enables Reformed believers to rejoice in the limitless power of God. Yet, in the same breath we are faced with the mystery of God, which lies beyond human comprehension. We experience God's mysterious power as Trinity, whose triune nature intercedes in our lives but exceeds our understanding. God is greater than our grasp; at the same time, the distance between us is narrowed by our experiences of God's grace. This in turn enables us to celebrate the divine presence in our midst, nurtured as we are from grace to grace, from mercy to mercy every moment of our lives. We Presbyterians believe we have no other guarantee in life than the reality of God's grace. Within the Reformed tradition, all experiences of genuine forgiveness and love are attributed to divine grace and mercy in action.

Presbyterians take pride in being realistic Christians. This is due to the Reformed belief that human nature is not perfect and that human achievements are not self-sufficient. From a Reformed perspective, all cultural and scientific "advancements" are subject to theological scrutiny. A reforming attitude toward the totality of life is crucial. In the spirit of "always being reformed," believers are challenged to question existing practices and innovations in the church and in society. Our freedom in Christ enables us to work for justice with love in a changing world. Our reforming stance also encourages us to be ecumenical in our outreach and concern for others.

Influenced by the Reformed tradition, Presbyterians take their work ethic seriously. Whatever our means of livelihood, our jobs and professions are viewed as a calling, a vocation before God demanding our best efforts. This attitude is at the center of Reformed understanding of stewardship. Influenced by Calvin's teaching, we are expected to view life as a process of holy living, exhibiting self-denial, seeking always God's will and destiny. What characterizes a Reformed Christian in practice is an unending passion for God's will; the Ten Commandments serve as benchmarks to guide our behavior. Obviously, most Reformed Christians fall short of the mark. Presbyterian realism therefore sees our lives oscillating between forgiveness and thanksgiving.

We are also encouraged to live a life of simplicity, to be savers and conservers of personal and natural resources. Responsible stewardship for Reformed followers ultimately leads us to a life of gratitude and generosity. We are primarily thankful for divine forgiveness personified in Christ. Through a spirit of thanksgiving and sharing we give glory to God, grateful that there is a divine purpose for each of us, whatever our circumstances in life. In the deepest sense, we see ourselves as the people of God called to be chaplains to one another, whatever our particular gifts may be, looking always to the Spirit's leading in the employment of our talents and resources.

While the historic development of the Reformed tradition is indebted to the Swiss Reformers, and especially to Calvin, no single definition of Reformed faith to this day has emerged to form a consensus. This is due in part to the tradition's reforming stance as reflected in our history of confession-making, exemplified in the Presbyterian Church (U.S.A.) *Book of Confessions.* Faithfulness to (1) the Word of God, (2) the sacraments, and (3) discipline are the distinguishing marks of churches within the Reformed tradition. Anchoring theological reflections in the Word of God (scripture) is the cornerstone in the formulation of Reformed beliefs, and the Bible continues to have an authoritative place in the shaping of Presbyterian reality today. The common ground in the Reformed tradition is the centrality of Christ. His life, death, and resurrection offer salvation from our alienation from God and neighbor. This is the message behind the symbols of baptism and the Eucharist. Our participation in these sacraments expresses our acceptance of God's healing power on our behalf. This is why the cross of Christ signifies hope at the center of our life together.

In the Reformed churches discipline is manifested through several forms of church governance: congregational, episcopal, and presbyterian. The word *presbyterian* actually refers to the practice of church governance in which clergy and laity are elected by the church and organized through judicatories at the local, regional, and national levels to enforce church order and discipline. The Presbyterian Church (U.S.A.) follows its ancestors in Scotland and England in its practice of representative governance, beginning through its presbyteries, and we owe much of our discipline to the Scottish Reformer John Knox (1514–1571). The forms of governance found within the family of Reformed churches all share a common Calvinistic heritage; internationally the churches of this Calvinistic heritage have been organized into a fellowship known as the World Alliance of Reformed Churches, which represents over 70 million Christians in 99 countries and consists of over 200 member churches primarily of Presbyterian and Congregational origin.

Reformed Christians do have their disagreements and unresolved issues. In the midst of debates within our extended family, we need to recognize that our tradition is not dead. A vital tradition embodies a conflict of interpretations. There is no absolute norm that satisfies all members of the Reformed family. A healthy family does not press for uniformity at the expense of testing ideas and a range of views. A split on one issue may cause turmoil, but in the midst of many issues a family can find space for agreement and disagreement on varied concerns while staying bonded together in love, mutual forgiveness, and hope, continuing to wish one another well in the journey of faith under the guidance of the Holy Spirit and by the grace of God, seeking always to be reformed.

Developing a Shared Vision

Congregational vitality calls not only for dependence on the grace of God, but also for a shared vision based on a common understanding of our heritage. Asserting the desire for ecclesiastical unity when conflict exists over apparently irreconcilable issues (for example, ordination of homosexual persons, or abortion), may not in itself have sufficient pulling power, unless there is common will among the members to be faithful to their heritage. Only as we are pulled together by an appreciation for the essential tenets of our past and their continued validity today will we be able to survive present ambiguities that cannot necessarily be resolved by a democratic process of vote taking. A congregational esprit de corps depends on a shared vision nurtured by a common commitment to the heritage that brought us into being.

Heritage creates a sense of family. This is what a denomination represents. It remains to be seen to what extent it is God's will that the mainline church families stay together despite their differing viewpoints. Within the Presbyterian tradition we are not expected to agree theologically and ethically on every issue; it is expected, however, that we will concur on basic matters of faith centered in the life, death, and resurrection of Jesus Christ. To agree on the essential ethos of our tradition provides a common ground to express our differences as a church family, praying that the Holy Spirit will lead us to a shared vision, much as Peter and Cornelius experienced (Acts 10), liberating us from our imprisoning positions that can easily sidetrack us from our primary mission.

The later ecumenical leader Lesslie Newbigin, known for his dedication to world mission, said that the church's primary mission today is the conversion of its surrounding culture. Our material culture, which pragmatically honors success and economic power, has become the real religion of our time, and it has penetrated all other religions. Philosopher Lewis Dupree of Yale University has noted that our culture offers the emotional benefits of religion without asking the price faith demands. According to Dupree, even those of us who are still in the church have become atheists, "not in the hostile anti-religious sense of an earlier age, but in the sense that God no longer matters absolutely in our closed world, if God matters at all."[5] Today this culture of ours with its own religious bent has imposed its agenda and its battles upon the church. What we are currently witnessing is the "de-energizing" of the church; we no longer seem committed to be the people of God, the body of Christ, worshiping, learning, and living out the good news of John 3:16 in the world.

Today's culture stresses reason, political muscle, and money to lead us to the promised land. The church, exhausted and weakened by these cultural battles, is unable to connect the grace of God it preaches to the human anguish that seeks healing and wholeness in our woundedness. To connect this human longing and hope to the divine touch of God's grace is what the mission of the church is all about. Every branch of the Christian church witnesses to this fact; as we look to our past with renewed zeal, we will place our differences into perspective, listening anew to what the Spirit has to say to the churches as we seek to be faithful as the people of God, the body of Christ. Nor can we overemphasize the church's primary agenda of reconciliation to God and to one another (2 Cor. 5:17–21); otherwise we will waste ourselves without furthering the kingdom of God where peace, justice, and love prevail.

As church members struggle to find common ground in the midst of their present battles with one another, it would be well within the self-interest of every church to rediscover its respective heritage and uncover the buried enthusiasm of its past. We will also confront our shortcomings, but in the overwhelming context of thanksgiving for the strides made toward revitalizing our church. Honoring our ecclesiastical heritage serves as a critical means of measuring our present efforts to be faithful as the people of God.

Discussion Starter

How much information does your congregation possess about its heritage? For instance, have you thought of starting a study group to read books written by Luther, Calvin, Wesley, or other significant writers in your tradition?

Chapter Four

Be a Welcoming Church

The Stranger in Our Midst

In my course, Church and Sacraments, for senior seminarians, a midterm assignment requires that every student attend and critique two church services outside of her or his particular tradition. The responses from members of these churches are usually wide-ranging, as the seminarians enter unfamiliar congregations as strangers. Some are warmly welcomed, others are seen as intruders, and the remainder simply encounter indifference.

At times, how a stranger dresses and appears influences how that person is received and welcomed by the congregation. One Sunday, Ed Dobson, pastor of the Calvary Church in Grand Rapids, Michigan, appeared at the three Sunday morning services of his conservative and traditional congregation dressed in torn blue jeans and a T-shirt, with his hair tied into a ponytail. As Dobson put it,

> I was preaching about how Christians get concerned about things that don't matter while not getting concerned about things that do matter. I preached the whole sermon without saying a word about my appearance. I talked about compassion for people in our community who are marginalized, disadvantaged—about breaking out of our circles of security.
>
> Finally, at the end, I said, "Now some of you today have been more upset about my ponytail than you are about people not getting Christ's gospel and Christ's love. The truth is, ponytails don't matter—but people do. I'm

going to cut my ponytail. What are you going to do about your neighbors?"
They remembered that one![1]

Some visitors feel as if they are invisible to the congregation. A few like it this way—they are comfortable with their anonymity and invisibility—but I suspect the majority welcome the recognition they receive and the fellowship after the service. Some strangers are even welcomed to a modest brunch after the service with a follow-up call and invitations to something specific in the next week. The depth of loneliness existing within our society is vast; it is not limited to our urban and suburban areas, but is found in small town settings as well. Most persons are waiting to be invited in a caring and authentic way.

Churches signal how welcoming and inclusive they are by the appearance of the facilities and availability of resources. Is our church neat and clean? Do we have a sense of pride in our church buildings and grounds? Are our restrooms working and tastefully decorated? Do we provide a nursery and is it well maintained? Is the narthex an inviting place to greet strangers? Is there adequate parking or have we made provisions at a nearby parking lot? Is the space for fellowship an effective area for community building? Do we make it easy for strangers to find us? How inviting are the road signs leading to the church? How accessible are we to the physically disadvantaged?

Most improvements to facilities cost money, of course, but to what extent have we explored creative budgeting through the volunteer talents of members and nonmembers? I don't know of a church that could not do *something* to improve its appearance to promote a more welcoming presence to outsiders. We can talk all we want about being a mission-minded church, but it often begins with attention to details.

In our cities and countrysides today many church buildings are no longer serving as churches. They have been converted into restaurants, townhouses, antique shops, furniture stores; I even know of a church building that now houses a brewery. The human spirit is creative and enterprising. It seems we have an abundance of churches that are skeletons of their former selves, struggling to continue. Churches can survive for a long time. Some survive because their church buildings were endowed by an earlier generation, enabling them to keep their doors open; unfortunately, they may be unwelcoming to the emerging neighborhoods in their midst. Other churches nostalgically long for the "good old days," and those lingering members remember the old neighborhood and tend to distrust the new residents on the scene. I suspect we have more concrete dedicated to God in our old neighborhoods than is spiritually healthy or pleasing to God. We must initiate a more welcoming spirit within our changing neighborhoods or we will become relics perpetuated and cared for by yesterday's endowment. This is why I believe church endowments are a mixed blessing.

The most significant endowment any congregation possesses is the living endowment of its people, who contribute not only their finances, but also their time and talent. Let's not give these parishioners any reason to believe that their input is less needed because of a legacy provided by earlier generations. Also, let us remind ourselves that today's dwindling inner city churches were yesterday's megachurches. Could it be that the present "seeker sensitive" megachurches might become the museums of tomorrow? It is quite possible that the current seeker's tastes will change, and if commitment levels are low, what assurance is there that a new generation will follow? There are some real challenges ahead for megachurches.

I am trying to suggest that a church's welcoming strategy needs to be more than an effort at being "seeker friendly." Taking clues from marketing research to recruit new members is not sufficient. Market research may indeed be necessary, as I noted earlier, but it will not ensure the continuance of our churches. A welcoming church is more than a public relations program or a sincere attempt to be seeker sensitive; a welcoming outlook is tied to a theological foundation that enables the church to encounter effectively the surrounding culture of death with all its fears and anxieties. The situation is further compounded by the violence we witness in the news and through television and film entertainment. Only a church with a resurrection outlook can overcome this culture of death.

However, if the church is either perceived or experienced as dying or dead, its members will find it difficult to have any hope for the church. In fact, if our own resurrection outlook is not articulated and our churches are less than lively, our efforts to be a welcoming institution will fall on deaf ears. We will become an increasingly invisible institution in society, no longer a prophetic voice for the enhancement of human life and the betterment of society. Our presence will be seen as making no real difference in society. As a witness to the living Lord, the gospel message of hope needs to point us to an alternative lifestyle, to meaningful relationships, and to a compassionate and caring God who promises us a more fulfilling way to live.

A Theology for a Welcoming Congregation

The apostle Paul instructed early Christians to

> Let love be genuine; hate what is evil, hold fast to what is good; love one another with mutual affection; outdo one another in showing honor . . . be ardent in spirit, serve the Lord . . . persevere in prayer . . . extend hospitality. (Rom. 12:9–13)

In the letter to the Hebrews we read, "Let mutual love continue. Do not neglect to show hospitality to strangers, for by doing that some have entertained angels without knowing it" (Heb. 13:1–2). These scriptural passages suggest a biblical theology for welcoming strangers into the congregation.

To begin with, a welcoming theology supports genuine hospitality. Actually, hospitality is not exclusive to Christians. Muslims, Hindus, Jews, and Buddhists are also encouraged to

56

receive strangers graciously. In his book, *Reaching Out,* the late Henri Nouwen proposed that it is obligatory for all Christians to offer open and hospitable space where strangers can cast off their strangeness and become fellow human beings. I have been a recipient of such hospitality on my numerous travels abroad as I recall events in India, Iran, Egypt, Korea, and China. My hosts were not always Christians. These experiences have been so important in making me feel at home in a strange setting.

The second aspect of a welcoming theology is to have some understanding of the stranger's situation and outlook. The most important step to building any meaningful relationship is listening. The stranger unfolds a story; we need to hear the unanswered questions within the narration. Are you in a position to assist with some partial answer that reaches out to the stranger's situation? Understanding always involves information, reflection, and engagement. The quality of our understanding is essential, especially in today's multicultural society where pluralism is a given factor in most of our communities. Everyone living with pluralism is struggling with questions related to their identity. The stranger who arrives on the steps of our churches may be no exception. How we listen to the stranger's story and the quality of our response may make the difference between hope and hopelessness for those who knock on our doors.

A welcoming theology of understanding requires time and the willingness to enter into a process of mutual discovery. Building trust takes time. Through such means of outreach the welcoming congregation becomes a community committed in love, understanding, and prayer for one another.

The third and final dimension of this welcoming theology is synthesizing. As we recall the most memorized verse among Christians, John 3:16, we see the importance of synthesizing. This verse has been recited so often that we may have overlooked its deeper message, that God loves not only the world, but everyone in the world. This is not always clear to us. Implied in this statement is the divine commitment to the *imago dei*—the image of God found in every human being. This is at the heart of the apostle Paul's preaching and teaching. It is also what we read in the letter to the Hebrews. This *imago dei* is implicit in everyone; this is why God loves the world and everyone in it. The task of interconnecting with all human beings is the synthesizing goal implicit in John 3:16.

The challenge to your congregation living within the awareness of today's pluralism is to be faithful to John 3:16 while practicing an inclusive welcoming theology, because God's imprint is found in everyone. In other words, a threefold theology of hospitality, understanding, and synthesizing has a single focus: to honor God's image in everyone. Such acknowledgment is basic to any welcoming theology that seeks to reach out effectively to a multicultural society where pluralism is very much a part of today's ecclesiastical landscape. The church's task is to proclaim the evangel (the good news of John 3:16) without encasing its obligation in narrow interpretations and practices of evangelism, which have threatened to undermine the evangel into another "ism," another ideology that is actually in competition with the evangel. Christians should be ever mindful of the tension between the evangel and evangel*ism*.[2]

Christians believe that God in Christ loved humankind. With this conviction as the foundation of our faith, we are expected to live up to the standards of our founder. Jesus as the Christ models for us in the midst of our inhumanity that authentic humanity is the act of forgiving love demonstrated on the cross of Christ. Even on the cross, Christ practiced hospitality toward the strangers on either side. His was an understanding love in the presence of violence, alienation, anxiety, and brokenness. For Christians, Jesus the Christ is the perfector and pioneer of our faith. His earthly pilgrimage confronted the inhumanities often associated with the status quo of our society. Jesus wants to free us from the self-imposed boundaries and customs that dehumanize us from one another. Today the Holy Spirit pushes us beyond those barriers, inviting us to take risks and cross boundaries for the sake of Christ.

We know that the future belongs to God, and we are encouraged to participate in that future.

To participate effectively, every congregation needs to articulate its mission internally and then share it publicly. The process of articulation is the synthesizing task so critical to a welcoming congregation. On a recent trip to England, I discovered a congregation that seemed to be doing this well. The congregation is St. Martins-in-the-Fields, an Anglican parish in the heart of London. It has devised a three-year mission action plan. Its mission statement is clear: "St. Martins-in-the-Fields exists to honor God, and to enable questioning, open-minded people to discover for themselves the significance of Jesus Christ."

Along with their mission statement, they have publicly declared and distributed a charter synthesizing their outlook. I include it here, for I believe it can serve as a model for other churches seeking to articulate their theological perspectives.

ST. MARTINS-IN-THE-FIELDS' TEN POINT CHARTER

1. We believe in and proclaim both the mystery that is God, whom we partly know and partly do not know, and the human need to worship.

2. We believe in and proclaim the person of Jesus Christ who distinctively reveals the nature of God and the meaning and purpose of life, and who calls us to follow him through the death of the cross to the place of Resurrection.

3. We trust in the Holy Spirit who prompts liberty, beauty, truth, love and joy against the waywardness of human nature.

4. We are committed to using the Bible in a way that takes account of all truth and relates it to the real experiences, both good and bad, that people have of life.

5. We are committed to a Church that conveys the Christian revelation in signs and symbols, particularly in the sacraments of Baptism and Holy Communion.

6. We are committed to exploring the meaning of the Kingdom of God and to making connections between what we profess and the way in which we live and work.

7. We draw inspiration from our patron saint St. Martin who, by cutting his cloak in two, demands that we look both at the resource we create and possess, and the way that it is shared.

8. We are committed to taking all people seriously wherever they might be at their particular point of understanding, while at the same time sharing with them whatever insights may have been gained by our relationship with God.

9. We acknowledge the destructive power of human sinfulness, and we welcome gratefully the forgiveness that God offers to those who are prepared to turn to the truth.

10. We are committed to identifying and affirming what is good and identifying and opposing what is evil, and living as best we can in the mess in the middle.

Every congregation looking for revitalization must declare its mission succinctly, and then outline the essential tenets that encompass its theological outlook and emphases. The congregation then should declare periodically its commitments through its liturgy. To strangers in our midst, this practice will clarify the basic character and beliefs that motivate the congregation to make a difference in the immediate neighborhood and surrounding society.

Are the Megachurches More Welcoming?

Are the independent, nondenominational megachurches more accepting of strangers than denominational houses of worship? From the point of view of "unchurched Harry" and "unchurched Mary," the answer is a resounding yes. The successful growth of these megachurches indicates that they are indeed more welcoming places for the unchurched. And as we know, these churches are increasing. The Willow Creek formula is now being employed by over 2,300 churches in fifteen countries through the Willow Creek Association and its affiliates. The average attendance in these emerging megachurches is four hundred or more, four times the national average of mainline churches. The Willow Creek Association hopes to have 16,000 churches within ten years. Is this the emergence of a new denomination? Time will tell.[3]

Megachurches are primarily positioning themselves to reach seekers. According to Alan C. Klaas, in *In Search of the Unchurched*, over seventy million unchurched people are living in the United States today. Interestingly, seventy to eighty-five percent of these unchurched people identify religion as important or very important in their lives. These people are mostly among the baby boomers and baby busters, between twenty-five and fifty years of age. The average age at Willow Creek Community Church in Barrington, Illinois, is forty; the average age of American churchgoers in the more traditional churches is fifty-five. Megachurches seem more willing to adapt than mainline churches in their desire to reach out to the unchurched. It will be interesting to see what happens when mainline churches make a greater effort at new church development in the next decade. How influential have megachurches been already on denominational new church development? The answer to that question will become evident when these new mainline congregations are fully functioning.

It is now becoming clear that the essential difference between megachurches and most mainline churches is not in the faith they proclaim but in how they proclaim it. Some mainline churches have begun Saturday night services similar to those at Willow Creek, complete with drama, avant-garde music, and a time for questions and answers following the message. Such services are meeting with success; they respond to one of the major causes that initially gave impetus to the megachurch movement, namely, the boredom the unchurched felt when they attended mainline worship services. Providing an innovative and more contemporary type service is one way for a traditional church to adopt a "new church development mentality" without compromising the core values and identity associated with mainline churches.

There are other lessons that mainline churches can learn from megachurches. One is to emphasize small groups. The megachurch slogan seems to be, "the bigger the church, the smaller it has to grow." Small groups address the human need for intimacy and a supportive community. The megachurch has often made more successful use of the gifts of lay leadership in their midst. The leadership core in most megachurches has uncovered what it means to be people of God in partnership. The mainline churches have a propensity for clergy domination; the megachurches seem to have established a better balance. Whether this can be maintained remains to be seen. Some, however, view the lay leadership emphasis as producing "religion lite" for the worshipers. How true this is requires further study and investigation. In the future, seminaries must play a greater role in developing lay leaders to study side by side with seminarians. This will do much to develop a healthier partnership for church leadership in the next century.

Finally, there seems to be a greater willingness on the part of the megachurches to invite seekers into their fellowship. The feeling is that the step from seeker to believer is better encouraged within the fellowship of the church where faith is more often "caught rather than taught." In any case, there is no denying the fact that an inviting fellowship of believers is an attractive welcoming sign to all strangers. This good news of welcome will spread widely in the community and beyond.

The answer to the question of whether megachurches are more welcoming is mixed. The answer depends on what your own church is doing on behalf of strangers. From my observation, the strangers who call upon us fall within at least five identifiable groups, and each requires special attention in our welcoming efforts. These groups are (1) seekers, (2) prodigal sons and daughters, (3) the wounded and marginalized in society, (4) dormant members (the alumni/ae of the church who attend at Christmas and Easter), and (5) those who are taken for granted, the regular undemanding churchgoers who hide their needs, the "strangers" in our midst. Being a welcoming church calls for designing a leadership team in every congregation to work with a task force of members dedicated to hospitality. Depending on the size of your congregation and the number of persons who can serve, you may need to adapt specific responsibilities for your local situation. We no longer can operate with our usual membership committee way of doing business if we seek to be a visionary and growing church in the next century.

Discussion Starter

What would be for you the essential characteristics of a welcoming congregation? What grade (on a scale of 0–10) would you give your own church for its welcoming efforts? Discuss the grade with others in your group.

Chapter Five

Promote Prayer

The Sacramental Power of Prayer

Prayer is at the heart of everyone's faith journey. The quality of our prayer life measures the progress of our pilgrimage. Our experiences at church ought to provide perspective and substance to our prayers, but "educated prayers" from the clergy are no more effective than the prayers of a novice.

When we pray we engage simultaneously in various dialogues with God; at one moment we express adoration and praise, in another thanksgiving and confession, in another we announce our sorrows as well as our blessings, and present further petitions and supplications before God. All prayers are premised on God's grace and freedom to respond to us. The believer trusts that God has our best interest at heart; it is for this reason that every prayer is uttered in the spirit that God's will, not ours, be done.

Eugene H. Peterson, well-known writer, scholar, and translator of scripture, believes that "the impulse to pray is deep within us, at the very center of our created being, and so practically anything will do to get us started—'Help' and 'Thanks!' are our basic prayers."[1] There is no "insider" language to prayer. "Prayer," he points out, "is elemental, not advanced, language. It is the means by which our language becomes honest, true, and personal in response to God. It is the means by which we get everything in our lives out in the open before God."[2]

It is not surprising then to read the Pauline admonition to "pray without ceasing" (1 Thess. 5:17). On our Pittsburgh

Seminary campus, the presence of a prayer room, regular chapel services, and prayers before classes, in faculty and administrative offices, and at the beginning and close of committee meetings are ways in which institutionally we attempt to follow the apostolic admonition. On a personal level, we are tempted to ignore this praying attitude toward life; we are too busy trying to make it on our own. Even as we study the sacred subjects of the curriculum, including classes on spirituality, we know there is a gap between where we are and where we need to be in our communion with God. Prayer is that elemental sacrament and mysterious link between us and God and is not dependent upon bread, wine, and water. Prayer is the most private sacrament between us and God.

To say that prayer is at the heart of our faith journey is to emphasize that we need to pray daily, individually and collectively. To pray without ceasing is both an activity and a state of being that engages our hearts, minds, and souls. Through prayer we can foster an atmosphere of expectation and excitement that will energize our personal and community life together.

John Calvin often saw the world as a theater pointing to God's glory.[3] To transform this world into the kingdom of God we must learn to pray with our eyes open as well as shut: open to the facts and insights gathered in the marketplace, and shut in meditation and awesome wonder before the mysteries of God, which defy absolute definition. These methods correspond to the two traditions of prayer in Christian history. Apophatic prayer is "praying with eyes shut," centering on the Divine in silence, knowing that all human expressions of conceptualizing are inadequate. Kataphatic prayer is "praying with eyes open," seeking to express in a limited way the majesty of divine grace experienced. Both approaches, at their deepest levels, view prayer as listening for God's peace and presence beyond words and images as one enters into a unifying moment of ecstasy and tranquility. Being at one with God (John 17) and listening to the murmuring of the Spirit within the silence of our hearts are the essence of prayer.

Praying is a universal exercise among all believers. Every tradition in its own way fights against turning prayers into form without substance. The late Rabbi Abraham Joshua Heschel said, "Great is the power of prayer to expand the presence of God back in the world."[4] But for Heschel, talking *about* God, which is what theological educators do, can become idle chatter unless one first learns to talk *to* God. Real prayer seeks to address God through silence, not chatter.

Unless we dialogue prayerfully with God, the study of scripture and theology will become arid. Prayer needs to be foundational to our lives if the excitement and enthusiasm for studying the sacred is to flourish. William James observed, "Prayer is the very soul and essence of religion."[5] It is more than the human attempt to bend God's will to our will, it is more than the human manipulation of divine providence, it is more than spiritual lobbying for our desires. Prayer instead quickens our sense of social responsibility and stewardship before God. Believing in a loving and gracious God, we ask for God's will to be done in our lives.

What we pray for and how we think about God are closely related. This is why theologian George S. Henry used a simple method to evaluate the writings of theologians past and present: he looked for what they said about prayer. If a theologian took prayer seriously, Henry took the theologian seriously, for he realized that prayer is the fundamental way we relate to God. This is why we must make sure that church education centers on God; we come from God, we are sustained by God, and our destiny is to be with God. Prayer is our way of expressing trust in God, finding affirmation as we move closer to the divine purpose and meaning of our lives. Augustine said, "We are restless until we find our rest in God."[6]

Prayer is also our means to combat the demons in our midst. According to Luther, prayer is necessary in our struggles with evil:

We know that our defense lies in prayer alone. We are too weak to resist the Devil and his vassals. Let us hold fast to the weapons of the Christian; they enable us to combat the Devil. For what has carried off these great victories over the undertakings of our enemies which the Devil has used to put us in subjection, if not the prayers of certain pious people who rose up as a rampart to protect us? Our enemies may mock at us. But we shall oppose both them and the Devil if we maintain ourselves in prayer and if we persist in it. For we know that when a Christian prays in this way: "Dear Father, thy will be done," God replies to him, "Dear child, yes, it shall be done in spite of the Devil and of the whole world."[7]

Following his forty days of fasting in the wilderness, Jesus used prayer to counter Satan (Matt. 4:1–11). Jesus was vulnerable at that moment and Satan knew it, tempting Jesus with offers of food, power, and wealth. Jesus, empowered through praying, responded each time with the aid of scripture. He was fully aware of the sacramental power of prayer.

Prayer is also useful in sidestepping the defenders of antiquity that seek to drag us down into irrelevance. Under the guidance of the Holy Spirit we need inspired and visionary prayers to lead us. Too many of our prayers seem to restrict us to the status quo, missing our need to minister to an increasingly hostile and hurting world undergoing rapid change. Church critic William Easum has noted that churches and theological institutions "with a slow pace of change are no longer adequate in a fast-changing world. Structures designed to coordinate ministry are unable to cause innovation. Ministries that worked in the industrial society no longer meet the spiritual needs of people in an informational society. In an age of computers, we cannot express truth in the language of a chariot age. The time has come for new wineskins."[8]

Visionary prayer is rooted in the recognition of change. And with that in mind Easum identifies seven assumptions Christians must make about the future, specifically the twenty-first century, that will be at the heart of visionary prayer:

1. North America is the new mission field.
2. Society will become increasingly hostile toward Christianity.
3. The distinction between clergy and laity will disappear.
4. If churches only improve what they have been doing, they will die.
5. The best way to fail today is to improve yesterday's successes.
6. Bureaucracies and traditional practices are the major cause of the decline of most denominations in North America.
7. Traditional churches that thrive in the twenty-first century will initiate radical changes before the year 2001.[9]

Easum exhorts us to distinguish between essential beliefs that need to be maintained and nonessential practices that we should shed. Haven't we already witnessed church buildings turned into furniture stores, restaurants, antique shops, and townhouses? Do we need further evidence to sound the alarm? Dinosaurland may already be upon us as we cling to "security," seeking institutional guarantees that cannot be made, and failing to remember that God's grace is our only guarantee in life. Today, institutional long-range planning is confronted with tough choices as churches and seminaries seek to clarify priorities; the call is out for a new re-formation within our communities of faith that is future-oriented and realistic. Canadian writer Douglas Coupland, author of *Generation X*, already anticipates the irrelevance of the church in his book *Life after God.*

Finally, the sacramental power of prayer will help us to develop the urge to find meaning, transcendence, wholeness, and truth. Prayer makes a difference in life by changing our view of the world and our understanding of ourselves. Prayer gives us a cosmic outlook beyond our limited horizons. Through prayer, this instinct to look for truth and meaning is given an opportunity to express itself; the channels of prayer can lift us to new levels of authenticity and fulfillment beyond our imagination.

In her book, *The Body of God*, theologian Sallie McFague has suggested that all the world is God's body. We are a network of humans who can empower one another by the grace of God through prayer. Spirit-led prayers are essential in quickening the pulse of our congregations, enabling us to fulfill our mission. Prayer groups are an essential means in this transformation as we reach to revitalize congregations by the power of prayer.

Prayer Groups:
The Parishioner's Workshop

Within our anxious society, prayer groups for seeker and believer alike can become applied workshops, dealing with one's faith and concerns. The struggle between belief and doubt can converge within the supportive fellowship of persons who can give intimacy, friendship, and encouragement to each other in their faith journeys.

Prayer groups are the "little churches" within the larger congregation. They foster bonding among those who covenant to uphold one another in prayer and to meet regularly. Each one supports the other in carrying out the church's witness in society, offering encouragement when tragedy strikes, and learning that we are in this faith journey together. Hopefully, out of sharing and revealing vulnerability, we discover our common humanity and ask for God's grace to support us above and beyond our expectations. In other words, we will pray and bond together, becoming "the angel" God wishes us to be. By divine grace, we can empower one another to reach out and fulfill the destiny God has appointed for us. I believe there is a divine will and purpose that God has for each of us (Rom. 8:28) and also for each congregation. To be fueled by this theological conviction in itself offers a vision of hope that energizes us to fulfill our present stewardship before God. An effective prayer group keeps us accountable to one another as the people of God, the body of Christ.

Our petitionary and intercessory prayers will also lead to discussions on the nature of God and prayer. For instance, does prayer actually change circumstances? We will find ourselves engaged in prayer seminars, theological workshops that provide space to wrestle with questions and to learn and pray together as we delve deeper in God's grace and frustration with our own finitude. We will find ourselves intellectually and emotionally struggling with Jesus' parable in Luke 18:1–8, where he compares God to an unjust judge. Jesus informs us that this unjust judge neither fears God nor cares for humanity. Through the widow's persistent petitions, the judge finally grants justice. Reflecting on this action, Jesus observes, "And will not God grant justice to his chosen ones who cry to him day and night?" (v. 7).

Is it possible to sway the eternal God with volumes of insistent petitions? This theological challenge confronts every prayer group. As theologian Ronald Goetz asks, "Where has God, the answerer of prayer, been in the modern world's killing fields—from Armenia to Auschwitz to Cambodia, to Bosnia, to Rwanda? Surely many of the victims prayed to God for deliverance. Why such maddening variations in God's responses? Enter the Unjust Judge—the electing God who can appear ruthless and arbitrary."[10]

The Variety and Benefits of Prayer Groups

Churches that promote prayer groups understand the power behind congregational vitality, the bonding that results from coming together to pray and share. Groups provide an opportunity to name our anxieties in the fellowship of believers. We empower one another and offer a sense of belonging. A faithful intercessory prayer group rooted in candor and confidentiality will enable members to lower defenses, express vulnerability, and provide some measure of safety in the closeness of caring persons. The following is the testimony of a woman in a prayer group:

One effect upon me of this intercessory prayer [group] is a greater interest in other people, especially the people I am praying for. On the whole, I think I have been kind to people and have wanted to serve others in the course of my life, but I have also tended to be shy, feeling rather unworthy of taking interest in others. Now, I am unabashedly curious about the lives of the people I pray for. I really want to know what is happening to them, what life is like for them, in order to get some sense of how God is working in their lives. I feel how much I want the best for them, first the people I pray for, and by extension, everyone I meet, and how deeply I yearn for God's Will to be done in their lives and to be able to see that Will at work.[11]

Prayer groups also help us to articulate our beliefs and indirectly influence us ethically as we face the market realities of our society. Ultimately, prayer groups teach us to maintain a conscious dependency upon God. Praying together enables members of the congregation to develop a shared vision for their church, and to admit once again that there is no need for any of us to be islands to ourselves. We are interconnected as we pray and uphold one another before God.

Prayer groups can be specialized within congregations, with groups based on vocational interests and common age; for instance, there are groups for homemakers with young children, Internet users, sports fans, clergy, professional managers, assembly workers, and senior executives, to name a few. In other words, the church ought to assist and encourage persons to join one or more prayer groups within the church, at work, or in the neighborhood.

The variety of prayer groups can be endless as we allow ourselves freedom to tailor these groups for specific interests, knowing that when they are functioning well they nurture and strengthen us in our onward journey of faith, ultimately transforming us into the communion of saints who have witnessed the vision glorious in its fullness.

Discussion Starter

How significant is prayer in your life? As we listen to one another's responses, what can we learn from each person? How can we go forward together in our journey of faith? Are you a part of a prayer group?

Nurture the Youth

Where and Who Are the Youth?

The aging of mainline churches today is apparent. Take, for example, the Presbyterian Church (U.S.A.): 67 percent of the membership today is at least fifty-six years of age. It doesn't take a rocket scientist to wonder about the church's future leadership and members. The vitality of tomorrow's church is dependent upon the engagement and enthusiasm of youth. But where are the young people?

No doubt there are many answers to this question. And the answers vary depending on which age group you are addressing. There has been a good deal said about the baby boomers (those born from 1946 to 1960) as a generation lost to the church. Although in the recent decade many have returned for the sake of their families (some especially attracted to the "seeker-friendly" church services), a majority still tend to be alienated from the church. Most of the children of the baby boomers are known as Generation X or baby busters; they are much fewer in number (45 million) than the 78 million baby boomers. The Generation Xers are actually hard to describe; their general outlook is amorphous, intangible, and elusive. That is probably why they are referred to as Generation X. We almost need to fill in the blanks on an individual basis. Yet, Generation Xers do worry about the future; it is a major source of stress for them. A vast majority of Xers say, "No matter what I plan for the future, when I finally get there, it's always something different."[1]

Some Xers opt out of the rat race, while others are driven to work hard yet do not equate success as their fulfillment in life. In fact, "Never confuse having a career with having a life," might be their slogan.[2] It is these Xers who have been put on guard by the recession of the 1980s and are largely planning a fulfilled life without God, at least without God as packaged by the church. They are mostly the twenty-somethings, many of whom are victims of broken families as well as economic recession. Their trust has been eroded deeply. They are latchkey kids; many have some sense of homelessness and do not necessarily see the church as a home in any sense. Many have experimented widely with drugs, sex, alcohol, violence, and compulsive shopping. "Life after God" for the Xers is wired to the competitive realities of the marketplace that requires them to compromise their principles to achieve success and security. Many Generation Xers want to duplicate the affluence of their grandparents, a much stronger drive than the idealism of their parents' generation. This down-to-earth pragmatic cynicism leads to a low level of commitment to all institutions. Job hopping more than company loyalty seems to be the pattern of their lives. This attitude carries over to the church as well: they tend to be cynical about nonprofit institutions but are surprisingly optimistic as individuals with a sort of "can do" philosophy.

The emerging group of youth has been referred to as "Generation Y," persons born after 1980 (though some surveys begin with 1976) and are 57 million strong in America today (if you begin with 1976, it would be over 72 million). They are larger in number than the Generation Xers but smaller than the baby boomers. Members of Generation Y see themselves almost on a different planet than their parents. Computer technology is a given for them; some produce term papers with full motion video. Nearly 60 percent of children in Generation Y under the age of six have mothers who work outside the home, compared with just 18 percent in 1960.[3] Correspondingly, 61 percent of American children between the ages of three and five attend preschool, compared with 38 percent in 1970. And nearly 60 percent of households with children aged seven or younger have personal computers.

The portrait of Generation Y is not complete without noting that the number of racial and ethnic minorities has increased greatly and, according to the Census Bureau, will comprise the majority of our elementary level students by 2050, compared to 22 percent in 1974. Already 15 percent of U.S. births in recent years are to foreign-born mothers, and a hundred different languages are spoken in the school systems of New York City, Chicago, Los Angeles, and Fairfax County, Virginia. Moreover, nearly one in three births in the 1990s is to an unmarried woman. With the divorce rate about the same as the birth rate, clearly at least part of Generation Y's childhood will be in a single parent home. Finally, one quarter of the children under six are living in poverty, defined as living with a cash income of less than $15,141 for a family of four. This situation opens the door to government programs and their abuse, and to potential crime to supplement income. Generation Y will grow up with a reduced fear of a nuclear war, but many will be without the benefits of the traditional nuclear family.

The parents of Generation Y are always searching for greater safety for their children. As a result, we have a number of large indoor sports arenas; the number of indoor playgrounds for children and youth who can afford them will increase. The computer will be another kind of playground as well as a learning tool. Generation Y will have a global mindset, with conversations carried out internationally through the Internet. Through this global networking, Generation Y will become increasingly aware of the growing gap between the haves and the have-nots in the world. They will be unable to hide under the parochial mask of ignorance about the larger world and its demands.

When we begin to add all this up, we can see where the youth have gone: following the example of baby boomers and Generation Xers, today's teenagers (Generation Y) do not give the church a high priority. This trend will continue unless a compelling case can be made to these young people (as well as to their parents and grandparents) of the church's significance for their lives. As these young people cross the threshold of the next century, we must help them grasp the role of a vital church in shaping and enriching the society they will inherit.

Can a Compelling Case Be Made for the Church?

What does the church in your community represent? Some believe there are too many churches competing for a diminishing number of parishioners. Others see the church as a place where the older generation gathers and where day care assists working parents. For many there is a growing impression that the church doesn't make a difference in society. Of course, there are those who disagree! Perhaps the vitality of your congregation is due to the visionary spirit that enables your church to make a major difference in the life and welfare of your community. I hope so; in fact, your congregation may be in the best position to offer a compelling case for the church. Many persons readily stand up and testify for Christ, but I have not heard nearly as many witness to why the church is important to them. Perhaps if more church members of all ages would articulate the church's value for themselves personally, we could unleash the exciting beginning of a shared vision for the church. And with it would come the most compelling case for your church's presence in the community.

As I reflect on compelling arguments to make for church attendance, my first position is pragmatic. The church stands for values that humanize society and reinforce respect for one another's intrinsic rights and dignity. As we learn to practice forgiving love toward one another, we will further humanize the marketplace and exemplify the church's message of reconciliation and good will.

Moreover, recent studies show that regular church attendance is beneficial to health. For instance, the Graduate School of Public Health at the University of Pittsburgh has approached Pittsburgh Seminary, where I teach, to establish a Consortium on Faith and Health. Persons who "regularly attend religious services have been found to have lower blood pressure, less heart disease, lower rates of depression and generally better health than those who don't attend."[4] Such a link between church attendance and health has practical value and points us to an understanding of wholeness and wellness of our total self—physically, psychically, and spiritually. Churches that hold healing services and prayer sessions do so not only for physical healing, but also for psychic and spiritual healing.

Another practical consideration that argues for going to church is to combat the social abuses in our society. For instance, it has been demonstrated that young people who attend church regularly have a reduced rate of crime. According to the Search Institute's findings, those involved in church activities have fewer drug problems (5 percent vs. 14 percent); less truancy from school (6 percent vs. 14 percent); are less sexually promiscuous (22 percent vs 42 percent); and engage in less binge drinking (18 percent vs 32 percent).[5]

However, from my standpoint, the most compelling reason for an intergenerational commitment to the church now and into the future is that we are incurably religious by nature. It might even be said that we are actually engineered for religious faith. Whether or not we go to church, we have a human propensity toward idolizing Someone or Something at formative periods in our lives or during crisis times.

It has also been noted that "religious progress" is made on the personal level by the denunciation of "gods" in our lives—those objects or persons that we place on pedestals and idolize until we find cause for disappointment and then abandon them, switching our devotion elsewhere or falling into despair. Perhaps this explains in part why some disappointed individuals are reaching back to idolize the legacy of Marilyn Monroe or Elvis Presley. On the other hand, the church witnesses to the biblical fact that there is no god but God who alone is deserving of our worship. Such a steadfast devotion inspires us to fulfill our created destiny to love God and to love one another as persons like ourselves created in God's image.

Through the church we gather to express our allegiance to God, whose will and wisdom give us direction and fulfillment. Of course, God is not limited to church buildings; one can express devotion to God in the sanctuary of nature, but it is God the Creator (not nature) whom we worship. Such worship and praise remind us that our identity is incomplete without God, and that we cannot be good without God's help. Without the grace of God we are incapable of the healing forgiveness that beckons us to experience salvation as wholeness of health now and into eternity. Going to church clearly reminds us that we cannot make it on our own in life.

For no matter how successful we are, we have also failed; the price of success often involves costly tradeoffs and broken relationships. The mercy of God pulls us through, and the power of God raises us above despair to remind us of our identity as God's children, offering a sense of fulfillment more satisfying than we could ever imagine or deserve. This is why I go to church; it places my life in perspective and provides peace beyond human calculations, with the realization that God's will is in my best interest. Jesus himself demonstrated for us the truth of this. He is the pioneer and perfecter of our faith; this is why Christ is at the center of the church's worship of God. The most compelling reason for me to go to church is to be reminded over and over again of these facts, to renew my faith and to place my life in the framework of God's abiding grace and love.

Youth Ministries: Strategies for the Future

There are many more qualified persons to suggest strategies for youth ministries; my days as a youth director are far behind me. But as one deeply interested in building a visionary and vital church, I know that the youth are a pivotal part of our future. And I believe there are eight strategies we must begin to implement immediately to ensure that youth become and remain part of the church.

1. Affirm and celebrate the youth who are already coming into our churches. This is first and foremost in any strategic planning for the youth. We need to listen to them, for they will give clues and suggestions about what needs to be included to have a nurturing and satisfying experience at church. They will also offer important clues toward building an effective Christian education program that will yield intergenerational benefits for all.

2. Your church's Christian education committee must include a significant number of young people. How often the youth are missing from our committee discussions! We need to realize that this is a joint partnership and the youth need to be involved in the planning. We must listen to them, and they must be a part of the decision-making process for implementing a successful youth emphasis at church.

3. There needs to be a leadership team of parents working with children and youth in their respective activities. One adult for every five young people in attendance would be ideal. Hiring a youth specialist will not do the job by itself; any sustained and meaningful youth ministry requires a leadership team of parents. I was deeply grateful during the days of my youth ministry to have enlisted a number of parents and single adults to work with me at church as a leadership team. This team effort became a bonding experience and a blessing for us as well as for the young people.

4. We need to provide strategic and well-planned field trips, retreats, and conference experiences. Young people often need to relate to adults other than their parents. Modeling, listening, and providing guidance are much appreciated by children and young people of all ages.

5. Don't be afraid to set up creative links among neighboring youth groups of other churches. Perhaps a cluster of smaller

churches can hire together a youth minister (or youth consultant) to serve all the young people in the area. Youth often like to be identified with a larger crowd than a smaller individual fellowship group permits. We err at times in isolating and being overly possessive of our young people, and thereby miss a greater vision for serving them. Likewise, there could also be creative links with responsible parachurch groups in the area. This needs to be determined on a case by case basis. And speaking of creative links, look within your own congregation for opportunities for interaction, such as inviting mature older adults to work with young people and children, inviting them to share their stories, talents, and wisdom from their life experiences. These can be enriching for all who are involved.

6. We need to develop imaginative and informative educational resources for our Sunday school classes and youth groups. Denominational offices will be helpful; in the spirit of ecumenism, we also need to be receptive to materials from other sources approved by the leadership team working with the young people. We should also explore and develop instructional materials for the computer, although the computer will not substitute for face to face fellowship and learning experiences together. On the other hand, computers can be a useful supplemental resource for young people who are geographically isolated or physically disadvantaged.

7. Theological schools need more actively to develop youth leadership courses for seminarians, clergy, and laypersons, as well as provide experiences on campuses for church young people. For instance, Pittsburgh Seminary recently held its first Summer Youth Institute with thirty-one young people from eleven states, nominated and recommended by their congregations. The institute was designed to provide an introduction to theological education for young people who have completed the eleventh grade. In essence this was a "theology camp," providing an opportunity to study the nature of ministry, similar to summer science camps. We hope this pioneering effort will be emulated by other seminaries. We plan to repeat our Sum-

mer Youth Institute, enabling more young people to explore serious questions of life. The seminary is an ideal setting to investigate these ultimate questions and to discover how leadership roles in the church can make a positive impact for good as we seek together to do the will of God.

Our message to these young people is simple: positions in the church offer exciting and challenging possibilities for ministry. We want to provide the "seed thought" of a possible vocational calling before God as a pastor or some other form of ministry offered through the auspices of the church and related institutions. From this experience, we hope that young people will gain a greater appreciation of what it means to be the people of God working together in a common calling to be the body of Christ.

8. Finally, theological schools need to establish professorships for youth and family ministries. This has already taken place in some schools. It is a need long overdue; hopefully, potential donors will step up to make it possible.

I believe all these efforts and more are essential in developing future strategies for youth ministries. Such ministries are crucial in building a vital church that not only addresses the needs of young people, but also transforms them into leaders of tomorrow's church in whatever calling they pursue as they seek God's will for their lives. Hopefully, today's youth, the people of God for tomorrow's church, will form a stronger partnership between clergy and laity than the church has ever known. Our future will require this if we are to address adequately the fast-paced changes and challenges of the twenty-first century.

Discussion Starter

Are you satisfied with your present youth programs at church? Why or why not? Outline an intergenerational theology that includes parents, grandparents, single adults, children, and young people into an exciting and fulfilling partnership.

Chapter Seven

Address Issues Knowledgeably

The Need to Reach Consensus

Is the contemporary mainline church in America preoccupied
with too many "nonissues" and therefore depleted of emotional energy and resources? According to theologian John B.
Cobb Jr., it is, and this condition has led to "lukewarmness"
toward the church.[1] While lecturing in South Korea recently, I
was given a message from Christians there that was simple and
clear: "Tell American Christians to recover their enthusiasm
for the church." In contrast to the rapidly expanding Korean
churches, we have become worn out, suffering from ecclesiastical fatigue for having wasted ourselves on nonissues. This is
precisely where we lack consensus today: Who determines
what is and is not an issue? The confusion and disagreements
on this question add to our lukewarmness and disinterest in the
church. Doesn't every individual and group in the church with
a cause think that their issue is worthy of the church's attention, time, and support?

Can any denomination with a diversity of interests and
members reach political consensus on what the essential issues
are? Perhaps we need first to build a theological consensus on
basic belief and then determine the social implications of those
beliefs for the church's public voice. To some extent we have
theological consensus on the essential tenets of the Christian
faith based on historic ecumenical creeds such as the Apostles'
and Nicene Creeds. However, when a congregation confesses
its beliefs and then considers the implications of these beliefs,

there is inevitably a clash of viewpoints, with the resulting voices emoting more than reflecting together. Why then are we surprised that all the noise from these "sacred assemblies" has so little impact in the social and political arenas? The civil rights movement of the 1960s was a significant exception in both church and society, and that struggle is not yet over. If we distance ourselves from advocating for our pet issues, we will find that we have seriously neglected the care and maintenance of our denominational structures.

How then can we engage effectively on public issues? Politicizing has taken our church's ship badly off course. For too long, many of us have taken our ecclesiastical ship for granted. Did we think we were on automatic pilot and could sail on indefinitely? We have now suddenly discovered that the church is running on only one engine instead of the full complement, and there is no automatic pilot. We are adrift without direction. Yet we continue our debates aboard ship as if all is well, not acknowledging the fact that we are leaking badly. With only one quarter of our steam power, and in desperate need of good maintenance, we seem bent on destroying ourselves. There is no captain at the helm wishing to take on the burden of a neglected ship with its cantankerous passengers and personnel.

Is the situation hopeless? Not if we act quickly and prudently. Now is the time to intelligently table our pet issues, whatever their nature, until we can address the underlying issue: getting this ship running again at full steam toward a clear destination and mission. How dare I suggest that we delay any longer the important issue that you are passionately pursuing! My suggestion may sound unchristian. Hasn't God called us to be prophetic and faithful before concern for institutions? Unfortunately, we have singlemindedly pursued this attitude in our denominations in recent decades, thereby becoming weak and lukewarm. We have not wisely integrated the implication of our beliefs with the ethical qualities of our life together. We have failed to educate effectively the membership on the importance of the church's public witness and advocacy. As it is now, who is going to listen to a sinking ship that has lost its esprit de corps?

It is imperative that we reach a consensus that our first order of business in the church is to revive a fatigued membership on a leaking ship. Otherwise, we are without an effective ecclesiastical base to be taken seriously in the world. Some special interest groups within our churches are already thinking of abandoning the mother ship and pursuing their own self-interests; those thinking in this manner are headed for an uncertain future. Furthermore, their absence will leave the rest of us poorer. What I am pleading for is both the expansion, not reduction, of our diversity, and the recognition that we need a well-powered ship that can run again on all its engines. Unless we are willing to suspend judgment about others' agendas and give our immediate attention to the repair of our ship, we will sink, no longer a viable means to further the kingdom. Perhaps it is in the best interest of the kingdom for our denominations to disappear. But are we ready to give birth to a new church, liberated from its past? Or are we willing to recover and implement the reforming nature of our church? Whatever our answers to these questions, one thing is clear: a church divided and without consensus cannot be vital.

Is there hope? Of course! If the church is indeed the body of Christ, then we must pursue the truth, trusting the lighted path that can lead us to be faithful to God. We must become again a learning church as well as a service-oriented church. Actually, learning and service nurture each other; we learn in order to serve, and as we serve we learn. The sanctuary is a good place to learn the realities facing society. To see the church as a worshiping, learning, and serving center can help us to pioneer change while uncovering a fresh consensus on many issues. As a result we will have fuller information on which to make better decisions.

Furthermore, any attempt to legislate through the church our self-interests prematurely (with inadequate knowledge) will lead to divisions within the household of faith. We will simply be contributing to our dysfunctionality as we continue to limp along on one engine. The church must be more of a fellowship of learners. How helpful it would be to envision the church as a Christian learning center, the yeast within the larger community, advocating enlightened and constructive change. Then the church would be the light on the hill, beckoning believers and seekers to taste the good life in Christ. As a learning church, we need to address selective issues knowledgeably as the people of God who realize that the truth will set us free.

Clergy as Followers: Empowering the People of God

For the church to be more of a learning center, we must make a greater effort to inventory the talents and accomplishments of our membership. We can then pull together more effectively for service in the community.

For tomorrow's church to have greater vitality we must allow its members to be the people of God (1 Peter 2:10). The clergy hold the key to unlock the vast resources the membership brings to the church. If the clergy are willing to liberate the laity from their limited and passive roles in the church, congregations will experience a new burst of energy and excitement. The church will widen and deepen its understanding of discipleship as congregations become more vital. There are already many examples of this taking place in churches of all sizes. Take, for instance, the leadership style that Dr. John Buchanan, senior pastor of the Fourth Presbyterian Church, brought to that downtown Chicago parish. He emphasized shared leadership, which meant a much greater degree of lay involvement, expanding the knowledge and experiences of the lay members to the church's benefit rather than concentrating simply on a centralized, staff-led administration. To this end, he designed an administrative system with twelve session committees, each with at least ten members, thus engaging dozens of church members and expanding the leadership base for planning and carrying out the dynamic activities of the church. This visionary step has led to a greater sense of vitality in the church, and has provided more leadership opportunities for women, minorities, young, and old.[2] This reorganization at Fourth Presbyterian Church has been an important key in enabling the congregation to further its mission within the inner city of Chicago. It has provided increased knowledge for the leadership team at the church, assisting them to minimize internal conflict as they address controversial social issues, and empowering the church staff to do much more through joint partnership with the congregation.

In the course of his ministry, Buchanan has discovered the importance of being a follower as well as a leader. Within any congregation, whatever its size, members have talents, knowledge, and wisdom that supplement the pastor's. Oftentimes, the question is whether pastors are willing to listen and enlist assistance. In practice, the role of leader and follower are interchangeable; knowing this, clergy and laity can be empowered to function in a healthier manner with greater vigor as the people of God, the body of Christ. In most churches today, however, there is a dysfunctional imbalance among the people of God; pastors have a tendency to centralize control and the laity tend to be passive, assigned frequently to lesser responsibilities. Some laity have even rationalized the situation by saying, "After all, isn't that what we are paying ministers for?" This imbalance has preempted congregational vitality and has caused many pastoral search committees to articulate their desire for a "super pastor."

This is no way to build a strong church or a national denomination from generation to generation. The succession of pastoral leadership in any congregation will inevitably be uneven; this is no fault of the seminary (although we wish for perfect students), nor is it necessarily the fault of the pastoral nominating committee that puts on its best face when presenting its imperfect candidate. We need to cease blaming one another as well as the ecclesiastical system of our tradition. Instead let's admit that we have not really lived up to our understanding of the church as the people of God. We have not empowered clergy and laity to work as equal partners on the bumpy highway leading to the kingdom of God. Our understanding of Christian leadership is simply too limited in scope.

Church history should have taught us that the church is too important to be trusted solely to clergy; likewise, it is equally true to say that the church is too important to be left alone to laity. Rather the call is for clergy and laity to be disciples together in a leadership team that works symbiotically, complementing each other's abilities and sharing accountability as it advances the church's mission. This is why I have not singled out clergy leadership as *the* panacea for what ails the church. It is too simplistic an approach organizationally, and it lacks biblical and theological support. Jesus chose disciples, and discipleship implies that the qualities for leadership and followership are both needed. Unfortunately, followership is often a neglected factor in the practice of professional ministry. The result has been an underdeveloped laity and ineffective team leadership in our parishes.

Robert Kelley, who teaches organizational strategy at Carnegie Mellon University, has identified certain characteristics of organizations in his insightful book, *The Power of Followership*:

> Leaders contribute on the average no more than 20 percent to the success of most organizations. Followers are central to the remaining 80 percent.
>
> Most people, however impressive their title or salary, spend more time working as followers than as leaders. That is, we spend more time reporting to people rather than having people report to us.[3]

Kelley observes that "followership and leadership are synergistic more than separate, and interchangeable more than caste-conscious."[4] Aristotle similarly taught that training as a nonleader was a necessary part of growing to leadership. Perhaps this is why for many a working definition of a leader is simply someone who can attract and retain followers,[5] because the leader is first and foremost a follower as well. As pastors make a more assertive effort at appropriate times to be followers vis-à-vis their laity, they will take a vital step in letting the people of God be the people of God. Herein lies a pivotal factor in bringing new life to a congregation. This can be especially meaningful in very small congregations that cannot afford a full-time pastor or in various "tent making" ministries within our business-oriented culture.

The Church and the Business World: Responsible Cooperation

How well does the church understand the dynamics of the business environment that encircles it? After all, the economic health of communities greatly affects local churches. Some churches have lost members as businesses have downsized and consolidated to meet the demands of competition and profitability. In such situations, what is the role of the church? Oftentimes, the people of God are caught between the forces of recession and recovery. Pastors are sympathetic to the unemployed in their parishes and communities; at the same time, decision makers in management argue for greater economizing and belt tightening. Caught between these conflicting forces, most clergy are confused about how to respond. When confronting such a vital issue in the community, the acquisition of adequate information and reliable knowledge for all parties involved is often seriously neglected. As a result, more emotion than wisdom is often expressed in the heated moments that follow.

Corporate management usually believes the church's involvement on behalf of workers is uninformed; yet pastors cannot be indifferent when parishioners are hurting in their midst. The church, after all, is in the business of compassion. Misdirected compassion, however, can be detrimental for the very persons the pastors are seeking to help. How then is the church to express its concern and care in a complex world? Fairness and justice as envisioned by most pastors and churches are at best approximations of the kingdom of God.

We live in a world of trade-offs, but we fail often to acknowledge that until a crisis appears. When a crisis looms, both business and church leadership (clergy and laity) must reexamine the cost of their positions. Certain trade-offs may be necessary when survival is at stake for any organization.

There is always a struggle when a trade-off affects lives. The anguish is often unseen; and the results may seem cold and unfeeling to the majority. Business leadership often fails to communicate the pain of their struggle, while at the same time responding defensively to church activism as naive. Church leadership in turn views business as callous. In most cases, neither perception is accurate. Each harbors a simplistic impression of the other. The knowledge possessed by any one party is incomplete.

This became clear to me recently when the troubled chief executive of a major business corporation called on me in frustration and said, "Why are clergy organizing unemployed workers and saying such bad things about the company? Don't they know the terrible suffering involved in our decisions? Why won't pastors listen? Why do they see management as the enemy? I'm a devout church member and a Christian. I resent what's being said and done by clergy. I'm really angry!"

This chief executive needs to remind himself that every action has a reaction. All acts reflect our self-interest, perceived and actual. Fact is often difficult to separate from fiction; the data at hand is usually incomplete, and our perceptions often unfounded. For example, in the case of the angry chief executive, his company was perceived as creating unemployment by investing the organization's resources outside the community. The actual situation was far more complicated than that.

Industry today is unable to maintain all the jobs it previously supported. We are living in a period of transition stimulated in part by high technology and increased global competition. John Naisbitt and Patricia Aburdene's book, *Megatrends 2000*, makes that amply clear. Companies are simply unable to turn the clock back to the "good old days." This is difficult to accept when management decisions weaken the worker's position. The concept of fewer jobs is difficult for any unemployed person to understand, even while he or she buys overseas products.

Management has the responsibility to explain its position, but explanations often come too late and tend to be less than candid. Top executives expect workers to sacrifice and retool their attitudes, yet often fail to show sufficient empathy, support, and sacrifice themselves.

For a company to explain difficult trade-offs and decisions calls for a different kind of dialogue from the traditional negotiating table approach of labor and management. A third party is needed, someone respected by both sides and thus able to initiate the process of unpacking the complexity of the situation and confronting the inevitable trade-offs ahead. The third party serves the role of "educator" and "pastor" for all sides, helping each to listen to the other's feelings and preventing stereotypical reactions. If there are additional possibilities and solutions, these will surface through the creative and resourceful guidance of a third party whose primary interest is a resolution of differences for the mutual welfare of all concerned within the community.

Such a third party needs to be sought and introduced *early* into the decision-making process if the listening skills are to have an opportunity to be effective. The traditional impersonal role of mediator or referee at the negotiating table may become increasingly passé. Trained third-party individuals known to the community are the wave of the future.

Every community has at least one or two respected persons who are trusted by all sides and who in turn value all parties. It could, of course, be a clergyperson, but not necessarily. Perhaps respected laypersons may be even more suitable. Perhaps a leadership team of clergy and laity might be best. The third party will be someone whom all the parties can accept, and who knows how to listen creatively. A believable third party can in a realistic and caring manner help all to face the inevitable trade-offs and to work for the most humane solution. Unfortunately, there seems to be no effective utilization of third parties today. Persons of good will, including the clergy and laity of the community, are often placed in a reactionary position following a disheartening management decision, leaving a trail of anger and disappointment within the community. Such conditions are not constructive to creative resolutions. The temptation for labor or management is to find quick-fixes, which may prove to be disastrous for the community in the long run.

The state of employment or unemployment within a community will always have a direct impact on the quality of life there. To enhance the quality of life for all ought to be the goal of responsible leadership in every community. Short-term solutions to long-term problems will never be satisfactory, regardless how politic it may be at the moment. The public and private sectors of society must be creatively engaged together; we need to see the emergence of a working coalition of management, labor, church, education, and government for joint problem solving on behalf of the total community. This five-way partnership is essential.

Every situation is complicated further by the political factors within organizations. Bringing insight and hope to these complex situations is really an art that we apparently have not been practicing very well. Church leadership in particular finds itself trapped between victimized workers and frustrated decision-makers, between those suffering from recession and those calling for painful cuts.

We held a symposium at Pittsburgh Seminary through our

Center for Business, Religion and the Professions on the pain of unemployment. Many people from labor and management came to express their hurts and concerns, and to seek answers. Unemployment is no longer limited to blue-collar workers. In fact, "blue-collar" and "white-collar" are not meaningful designations according to the Labor Department. When you are unemployed, you are unemployed! The question of one's identity, as well as putting bread on the table, is at stake for every unemployed person. Take the supervisor of a plant who finds himself unemployed overnight, but who loves to work. He is fifty-five, too young to retire, and not wealthy enough. He is too proud to go to his pastor to discuss his situation. Or look at the business executive who knows she is vulnerable and could be in the unemployed ranks overnight. She may not have immediate financial worries, but her self-esteem has been crushed. Some churches have formed committees to assist the unemployed, as well as to establish food pantries. However, churches are discovering that many persons are too proud to admit they need help.

The church must not only be involved in helping dislocated persons, but also in assisting management faced with the question of business suvival. Possible trade-off options not earlier considered could ease the pain of unemployment. I believe that the church needs to be brought early into the process of management decision making before battle lines between employers and labor leaders are formed. Clergy and laity can be trained through education and experience to become effective third party leaders in activating the moral imagination within a community.

Church leadership, not afraid to face conflict situations and angry voices, can challenge status quo approaches in times of recession and recovery. What our theological seminaries require today are faculty chairs in leadership, not administration. We have too many administrators and too few leaders among the clergy and laity in our churches. Perhaps we need to take our cue from the professorial chair in leadership established not long ago at the Harvard Business School, made possible by a gift from the Matsushita Electric Industrial Company. It is noteworthy that a Japanese corporation had the insight to offer such a chair to a prestigious American university. Where is the vision for similar initiatives on behalf of seminaries?[6]

Trained third party leadership, as I envision it, can assist those engaged in decision making to (1) identify and separate primary from secondary issues, (2) focus on primary issues without getting sidetracked in emotion, (3) stimulate the moral imagination of everyone involved to identify what is negotiable among the possible scenarios, and (4) develop a strategic plan of action based upon a broad level of support. Sacrifice and hurt may be unavoidable, but they can be reduced greatly when there is shared ownership in the decision making process and when there is an honest effort to face a significant issue with knowledge and sensitivity. A consensus among persons with common vision overcomes narrowly perceived interests and promotes the pioneering spirit on behalf of the larger community to achieve economic viability for the area. I believe that qualified clergy and laity can play a vital role in this process and that congregations will be invigorated by such involvement.

Discussion Starter

What current issues in the church are nonissues for you? Would others agree with you? Can consensus be reached on a list of common concerns? How knowledgeable are we regarding the concerns we debate in the church?

Chapter Eight

Practice Forgiveness

Christianity as Forgiveness

Some understand the Christian faith as forgiveness personified in Christ. This forgiveness centered in Christ has the power to humanize our existence. We live mostly in an unforgiving society, but if we could learn again the basic elements of the Christian doctrine of forgiveness, both our individual and social lives could be renewed. The church should be the house of forgiveness, for it is the role of the church to teach, preach, celebrate, and practice the message of forgiveness within the world. The meaning of forgiveness within the Christian faith can be understood in the following seven ways.

1. *Forgiveness as judgment.* The incarnation, God with us, is in actuality divine judgment upon us. Jesus' coming acknowledges our estrangement from both God and one another. His presence is evidence of our history of disobedience before God and points to our prideful, rebellious wills, which have caused us to be unfaithful, resulting in our separation from the very source of our being in God. Sin is essentially a broken relationship between us and God, a state of separation.

Divine forgiveness assumes the existence of sin. When we view forgiveness as judgment, we acknowledge that we are helpless in overcoming the human history of sinfulness, our distance from God. No means of corrective behavior, discipline, or punitive payment can rectify the situation. The option acceptable to God is that we receive humbly the gift of forgiveness as judgment upon us. All other efforts to overcome our estrangement are doomed to failure. Only God can close the distance between us, accepting us with our imperfection. The story of the prodigal son (Luke 15:11–32) is an illustration of this forgiveness as judgment and acceptance; the waiting father is reunited with his sinful son. Forgiveness assumes waiting as well as separation.

2. *Forgiveness as love.* Just as forgiveness assumes separation and waiting, it also assumes love. Forgiveness originates with God who loves us in spite of our sinfulness; it is love in action. This can be illustrated through the story of the prodigal son. The prodigal's father was ready and waiting in a spirit of love when the lost son returned. The visible embrace of the father and son was preceded by the father's forgiving love.

Theologian Søren Kierkegaard may have been thinking of the parable of the prodigal son when he wrote, "By *forgiveness* love hides a multitude of sins. . . . I *believe* that what is seen has come into existence from what is not seen; I see the world, but what is not seen I do not see; that I believe. Similarly, in *forgiveness—and sin—*there is also a relation of faith of which we are rarely aware. . . . Just as one by faith *believes the unseen* into what is seen, so the one who loves by forgiveness *believes away* what is seen. Both are faith. Blessed is the believer; he believes what he cannot see; blessed is one who loves, he believes away that which he indeed can see!"[1] Forgiveness as love points to the greatness of God's compassion, which ignites the forgiving process beyond human understanding.

3. To speak of forgiveness as judgment and love is to understand *forgiveness as grace.* The good news of Christianity is that the guilt originating from our sinfulness has been cancelled by God's grace. This was Martin Luther's great discovery. Weighted down as he was with guilt and anxiety, he had lost sight of God's miraculous grace. Luther rediscovered that the believer is accepted on faith alone through the grace of God; this is the evangel, the good news of the gospel. Theologian Paul Lehmann expressed it as follows:

Man exists altogether by the grace of God. When man is forgiven, he is forgiven in *toto* and from *moment to moment.* The consequence of the discontinuity between God and man is that God forgives man as the sheer miracle of his love and that when he forgives, a man's whole existence is changed. Changed?—yes, but not as simply moving from one house to another. Forgiveness, coming to man as the crisis of his existence, is a thoroughly paradoxical event. It is the paradox of the man who is both sinful and righteous.[2]

4. When we understand forgiveness as grace, we also come to understand *forgiveness as pardon.* The significance of this pardon, or justification by faith, is acknowledged almost universally by Christians in today's ecumenical era. The dependence upon God's grace limits all explanations as to how pardon takes place. Try as we may through traditional explanations of the atonement (sacrifice, commercial transaction, substitution, example, love, forensic), the fact remains that there is no final interpretation as to *how* we are pardoned from our sinfulness. The mystery of salvation is beyond rational explanations; we cannot know the divine plan. H. R. Mackintosh, in his classic book *The Christian Experience of Forgiveness,* expresses the limitations of our understanding by saying that "how God makes forgiveness real is hidden from us, and no enlargement of human faculty is conceivable for which the mystery would be resolved. . . . Events of vast spiritual significance—and every instance of Divine pardon, if it occurs at all, is such an event—cannot be wholly judged by narrowly rational canons which appear sufficient for simpler cases."[3]

While forgiveness as pardon is shrouded in mystery, justification by faith, implicit in the Christian understanding of pardon, involves a forensic dimension. To be justified or pardoned assumes that our wrong (debts) have been graciously cancelled (forgiven) by God. This cancellation points to the satisfaction of a forensic relation between us and God. Divine forgiveness discharges (pardons) us from our debts; believing this, we are justified by faith, by God's grace.

But a pardon from God is more than divine amnesty waiving the claims of the law. Divine pardon or justification by faith teaches that God accepts us not by waiving the claims of divine law, but by satisfying those claims as the divine purpose is made concrete in the life and ministry of Jesus the Christ.[4] This is the heart of Paul's teaching in Romans 3:21–31; forgiveness as pardon justifies us before God, while at the same time the demand of God's law is met.

5. When we experience pardon, a sense of relief enables us to experience *forgiveness as freedom*. As Paul indicates, Christ has set us free from the law of sin and death (Rom. 8:2). The freedom offered by Christ is real freedom (John 8:36). As the load of sin and guilt is lifted from us, we are able to free ourselves from the chain of events that has thus far controlled our existence. The freedom Christ offers originates in another realm; it contradicts and overthrows the laws and restrictions of this world. The freedom Jesus taught and modeled through his life was a threat to the powers of his day.

6. *Forgiveness as costly reconciliation* is well documented throughout the New Testament. There is a cross at the center of the Christian faith. From Jesus' birth to the cross, reconciliation initiated by God was a costly affair (Phil. 2:5–11). We worship a suffering God, as Jürgen Moltmann has reminded us, as did earlier theologians such as Horace Bushnell, H. R. Mackintosh, D. M. Baillie, and Leonard Hodgson.[5] Somehow God suffers, is not passive, and experiences the pain that sin brings.[6]

There are both vertical and horizontal dimensions to costly reconciliation. Vertical reconciliation requires God's suffering; this suffering began prior to the incarnation. Horizontally, the suffering is in the acknowledgment that we cannot forget the wrongs done against us by our neighbors as we go through the painful process of taking the first steps toward forgiveness. Unlike God, we are unable to forget the wrongs committed to us or by us. The cliché "forgive and forget" is not possible, Christian, nor biblical. Only God is capable of erasing our sinful histories (cf. Pss. 25:7, 79:8–9; Jer. 31:34; and Isa. 1:18). Biblically we are called upon to forgive in the spirit of God's forgiveness of us. The accent is upon forgiving, not forgetting.[7] Even if forgetting were possible, we would as a result find ourselves radically cut off from the past, and in a state of amnesia. Instead, we are asked to remember the cost of God's mercy through our participation in the sacraments of baptism and communion. As we receive and remember God's costly mercies, we are motivated to practice costly reconciliation with others.

"Forgive and forget" calls us to do the impossible, but God expects us to forgive without forgetting. That is why forgiveness involves a painful process. There is a cross at every forgiving encounter; open wounds take time to heal. Forgiveness without forgetfulness is the human way of loving one another.

7. *Forgiveness as healing* directs us to the goal of wholeness. The healing process points to wholeness, which begins with forgiveness. Paul Tillich suggested this in his sermon, "To Whom Much Is Forgiven," when he indicated that forgiveness is an event of joy and healing, "the greatest experience anyone can have. It may not happen often, but when it does happen, it decides and transforms everything."[8] The greatness of the forgiving event lies in the fact that it enables the creative powers of healing in us to be released. Any participation in forgiveness is a healing and uniting experience with God and with one another. The human face of God in Jesus manifests a healing and humanizing ministry of forgiveness. This humanizing power is the loving Spirit of Christ that heals and makes us whole. The paralytic ordered to take up his sick bed and walk away was both forgiven and healed; this incident represents God's intention for us all.

To recognize forgiveness as healing is also to admit that we cannot heal or forgive ourselves. Rather, the source of healing and forgiving is God. The initiative always belongs to God; the source of healing resides outside of ourselves. This divine factor reminds us that we exist from grace to grace, from mercy to mercy, every day of our lives. The healing aspect of forgiveness reminds us of our fallibility and fault. Having been forgiven from our sins, as Langdon Gilkey indicates, "we may more hopefully embark upon becoming like Jesus to our neighbor in the world. Thus the cross is not only a sign of the negation of the world, but also necessarily a symbol of the negation of the virtue of the prophet himself."[9] The healing process informs us that we are neither virtuous nor heroic; we are simply travelers, wandering, and oftentimes lost, but nevertheless drawn to follow, however imperfectly, the master of forgiveness incarnate.

Forgiveness is more than an individual matter; it is a corporate affair involving the structures of society. The corporate dimension of forgiveness in our theologizing frequently receives only a passing nod, but as Jesus was being crucified he said, "Father, forgive *them*; for *they* know not what *they* do" (Luke 23:34 KJV, emphasis added). Wherever corporate forgiveness exists, we have the beginnings of true community. Theologian Joseph Haroutunian once said that "the church is where forgiving neighbors exist."[10] The church as the forgiving community should be the harbinger of a forgiving society.

At the core of Christianity lies the doctrine of forgiveness. Responding to divine forgiveness and practicing forgiveness ourselves can humanize us. We are thus enabled to complete our incompleteness and to live and work toward a forgiving society.

The Sacramental Power of Forgiveness

It ought to be clear that forgiveness has profound implications; it is not a simple undertaking. Forgiveness as judgment, love, grace, pardon, freedom, reconciliation, and healing converge when we celebrate the sacraments of baptism and communion. These are the sacraments of forgiveness, where the mystery and meaning of our lives come together and when we realize anew that we are the children of God. This is why it is important for a congregation's vitality that these sacraments are practiced regularly and where all who confess their faith in Christ are given an opportunity to participate.

I believe it is especially helpful to have members reaffirm their baptismal vows annually, to understand again what it means to be baptized into the life, death, and resurrection of Jesus Christ. Our bonding with God through baptism has with it an implicit covenant of accountability not only toward those being baptized, but also toward all the people of God. We need to have a sense of responsibility for one another's nurturing sense of discipleship as we follow Christ, who while on the cross uttered neither a complaint nor an accusation, but a prayer: "Father, forgive them; for they know not what they do." The gospel according to Jesus is one of forgiveness; the church that witnesses in his name can do no less. The sacraments we celebrate remind us that forgiveness is at the heart of the Christian faith. To call ourselves Christians means not only to accept God's forgiveness on the cross, but also to practice forgiveness as Jesus taught his disciples through words and actions.

Sadly, many of us do not believe forgiveness is realistic today. How then can we expect the power brokers of our global society to take our faith seriously? What do we think life would be like without the possibility of forgiveness? I know what my answer is—hell! And many people (more than I like to think) are living in hell today, refusing to cross the emotional barrier of alienation, filled as they are with guilt and hatred, as they search for opportunities to destroy their so-called "enemies," created in God's image as they are.

The cross of Christ hovers over the global community today. As Christians we are bearers of the cross, and through the pain of forgiving we can help others to discover the therapeutic power and freedom that comes with forgiveness. Yet it is difficult to break out of our self-imposed prisons of hatred or animosity, which at times seem to bind people together. Too much of our energy and emotions are lost through hatred and misplaced suspicions. We are all in need of liberation and new life.

The idea of forgiveness, however, seems to fall on deaf ears in a cynical society that stereotypes its enemies and rationalizes its own behavior. Ours is a culture of victimization and blame, so it is all the more moving to witness a public act of forgiveness such as took place between the late Cardinal Joseph Bernardin of Chicago and Steven Cook, who in 1993 falsely accused Bernardin of sexually abusing him in the 1970s. At their two-hour meeting, Cook apologized and the two became reconciled. Together they celebrated a private mass for Cook and a gay friend. "I think I have grown spiritually as a result of this," said Bernardin.[11] Both ceased to be victims through this process of reconciliation.

A Postscript on Forgiveness

Since I believe forgiveness is the defining characteristic of the Christian faith, I share with you my personal statement in the hope that it can help you to reflect for yourself on what it means to be counted among the people of God, the body of Christ working to revitalize your church.

A Framework Of Christian Reality And Good News

I believe in a forgiving God in human history. I believe the cross of God in Jesus Christ is the signature of divine forgiveness for all time.

I accept the scriptures of the Old and New Testaments as the authoritive witness to this forgiveness.

I am persuaded to accept this divine forgiveness through the activity of God's Spirit, who beckons us into the circle of forgiving love.

I believe the church is the fellowship of the forgiving and forgiven. We confess therefore our imperfections and sinfulness individually and collectively. Dependent as I am on God's mercy, I declare my need for constant renewal and reform.

I believe the fellowship of the faithful is called to be creatively involved in overcoming the broken fragments within our global village. I am reminded of this calling through the practice of baptism and communion, sacraments of our brokenness and need for forgiveness.

I witness to the fact that earthly death is not the end. I believe in the crucifixion and resurrection of God's Son, who ushers us into a new society of faith, hope, and love.

I see signs of that new society when relationships are restored and new beginnings of compassion and justice transpire in our communities.

Discussion Starter

What is the defining characteristic of the Christian faith for you? Do you believe your church practices Christian forgiveness? Give examples of forgiveness, or of lost opportunities for forgiveness.

Chapter Nine

Work for Peace and Justice

The story in the first two chapters of Genesis depicts the Garden of Eden as the perfect garden, where humankind and nature lived in harmony. We glimpse that harmony when we listen at night to the diverse sounds of insects and other creatures being orchestrated into nature's symphony. Harmony assumes dissonance and diversity, a creative blending of sounds orchestrated to make our lives interesting, not boring. God invited us to delight in this garden and to care for its variety, directing us to live at peace with ourselves and with all of creation. As the biblical story unfolds, however, we express our freedom by becoming dissatisfied with perfection. As a consequence, our human story ever since has been one of suffering and adaptation to our imperfect status; exiled from the garden, we are lost. Is this our destiny? Are we sojourners searching for a return route to our perfect home?

Living East of Eden

Each of us lives east of Eden. Many of us see ourselves wandering through life without a destination, concerned only with the here and now. The only games for keeps are the temptations and trials of this present life. Eternity is a vague concept beyond comprehension; at least it is beyond the scope of present technology to capture on the screen of our imagination.

Within this limited universe of measurable realities, we learn to make our way, to teach our offspring, as did our forebears, how to survive and defend themselves. Survival dictates that we be somewhat selfish as we look after our best interests. In time, we claim that greed rather than generosity may be the best policy to ensure personal, tribal, and national survival, since natural resources are not endless. We pass on this attitude; those who feel otherwise often do not succeed in this harsh world. We wish it could be otherwise; we wish that generosity would win in the end, but we are afraid to take that chance. We may be believers, but we are atheists and agnostics in practice. Our interests and our neighbors' interests are in a tug-of-war when resources are scarce, and we seem to want more and more. Living with conflict and violence seems to be inevitable east of Eden. Do you think this is the situation the writer of the epistle of James had in mind?

> Those conflicts and disputes among you, where do they come from? Do they not come from your cravings that are at war within you? You want something and do not have it; so you commit murder. And you covet something and cannot obtain it; so you engage in disputes and conflicts. You do not have, because you do not ask. You ask and do not receive, because you ask wrongly, in order to spend what you get on your pleasures. Adulterers! Do you not know that friendship with the world is enmity with God? Therefore whoever wishes to be a friend of the world becomes an enemy of God. (James 4:1–4)

James's words offer a window through which we can recognize our present situation. To work for peace and justice under God promises difficulty and requires discipline as we take each step under the guidance of the Holy Spirit, the source of life who channels the flow of grace on our behalf. Living east of Eden, we are dependent upon God's grace; we have no other guarantee in life as we struggle with the destructive forces of evil. It will never be easy; and it cannot be done without divine empowerment as we unmask the false images of God. We long for affirmation as we transform a crowd of lonely strangers into a community of caring love, seeking one another's welfare.

To reach this vision of society requires individual risk and responsibility.

Guidelines for Advancing Peace and Justice

To advance peace and justice, we must first identify those universal convictions and values worth preserving whatever the cost. We must make this determination through balanced discussion in both our churches and also publicly through town meetings, the workplace, governmental agencies, and the judicial system. We must understand political processes in order to ensure a fair hearing to clarify the substantive values being discussed. We must all do our homework as we listen to a range of viewpoints on the issues under discussion. To succeed, we can use the following three guidelines for our work in the church.

Guideline One:
Seek Out the Image of God in One Another

This guideline requires us to uncover and respect the divine birthmark in each person, for we are all created in the image of God. This implies that we must hold one another accountable to that divine image, difficult to do in the midst of highly charged battles where we might deeply wound and kill relationships, turning at times our verbal fights into violence. We cannot afford to lose our civility; our high calling is to respect the intrinsic worth of the other, in spite of our intense distaste for the "enemy" who seemingly has abandoned the image of God. It is this invisible image of God, this theological thread of faith that knits human beings to one another. By God's grace we must continually work to uncover that spiritual factor. The best means to strengthen that theological thread among us is through the practice of forgiveness, discussed in chapter 8.

The tough ethics of forgiveness cannot be ignored in the heat of debate where human emotions are unbelievably strained. Ethicist Donald Shriver recognizes this:

> People who take the trouble to listen to each other are vulnerable to empathy, and the path to empathy lies through forbearance. For the moment none of us may know what truths or principles we should learn to applaud in the brew of our cultural diversity. We may not yet grasp with confidence the moral judgments that we will eventually make about our past and present relations with each other. We may lack the empathetic knowledge of others necessary for making settled judgments about them. Meantime, the forbearance that says "let us not leap into retaliating against each other" and empathy that says "we are beginning to understand why each of us feels the way we do" is a solid prelude to real politics. For politics is the struggle of diverse groups and interests to fashion common action on some common agenda. Without the time and patience for discovering that agenda, we leap to inept conclusions, and the day of realistic politics never comes.[1]

Implicit in Shriver's comment is the principle of human worth, upholding the image of God, no matter how absent it might seem at the moment of battle. However, upholding the image of God in one another does not mean that we are obligated to practice unlimited tolerance toward the "enemy" who might be committing terrible harm and evil, for, as Shriver points out, "Civic diversity is not the same as infinite tolerance."[2] For instance, given its history, Germany bans neo-Nazi political parties. Our American democracy strongly endorses individualism and freedom, so it is unlikely that even such hate-filled groups will be restricted in the United States. Yet as Shriver points out again, "human beings cannot remain neighbors in a society of unlimited literal 'freedom for the thought we hate,' especially when that thought takes the form of denying to others their claim to justice as well as freedom."[3]

In our zeal to be tolerant, many mainline Protestants have drifted into what psychotherapist Michael Maccoby calls a "soft humanism where faith is lost and with it the passion for transcendence which most people need to sustain a strong humanitarian spirit of service. An undiscriminating tolerance in a desire to avoid rigidity and exclusiveness, undermines believers' yearning for transcendence, substituting relative and tentative 'commitments' based on pragmatic considerations rather than principles based on faith."[4] In our ardor to be tolerant for its own sake we are in danger of losing the foundation of tolerance rooted in our understanding of the image of God. All of this is to say, we must be on guard lest we slip into a practice of uncritical tolerance, condoning and practicing what is inherently evil. As believers in the image of God, we are to uphold human dignity in all circumstances, "learning enough about each other to discover the benefits of difference—as well as the bonds of commonality."[5] Functional democracies and local congregations depend on both for their healthy growth.

We ought to celebrate then the worth of every person created in God's image, which is the biblical premise that enables us to seek justice in matters of racism, gender and age discrimination, sexual orientation, and numerous other issues. At times we get so mired in the details and procedures of debate that we lose sight of the biblical norm, accusing one another of manipulation, guilt, heresy, and wrongdoing. My experience is that in all keenly felt justice issues, we need to maintain a painful process of forgiving while dialoguing, lest the scars of the past overcome us and prevent the possibility of reconciliation. If we do not, we will have injured personhood for the righteousness of our cause, making forgiveness and healing nearly impossible. The healing of relationships comes slowly and is only possible if our wounds are bathed and baptized in the clear, healing streams of God's forgiving and accepting love.

To uphold God's image in one another is a mandate throughout scripture, articulated in the Ten Commandments as well as in Jesus' summary to love God and neighbor. These are God's rules of behavior for us. Vital congregations must articulate for themselves, as well as to the larger community, the heart of God's expectation based in scripture. A recent survey conducted by the *Wall Street Journal* and NBC News found that Americans continue to be strongly supportive of religious teachings. Almost a third of the respondents of this poll indicated that "beyond having a good family, a strong religious faith was the best indicator of a person's success. When it comes to issues of right and wrong, 37 percent of respondents said they should be decided based on God's law. Only 25 percent thought they should be decided by society as a whole; and 33 percent said they should be a matter of personal conscience."[6] The church must proclaim in the public square unapologetically the importance and relevance of these biblical standards.

On the other hand, we must not allow scripture to be manipulated to support the particular self-interests of any group. Both sacred and secular history illustrate such abuses in defense of ideologies and political agendas. Such abusive practices will get us nowhere beyond fighting and wasting our energies. Yet this is what we have been doing in the mainline churches, and we are weaker today because of it.

Unfortunately, today we often misuse scriptural authority, overlooking history and its use of scripture to defend slavery and segregation, to exploit workers, exclude women, justify poverty, support greed, and abuse the environment. Scripture is authoritative and instructive when it is not manipulated according to our biases, when we can appreciate its essential guideline: to maintain the divine image in one another and hold one another accountable as we build the body of Christ in order to do justice and to walk humbly with God and our neighbors in peace.

Guideline Two:
Uphold the Sanctity of Nature

The second guideline toward establishing peace and justice is to recover the sanctity of nature. God created a garden of beauty with all forms of life and invited humankind to be responsible for it. Human sin is seen in our irresponsibility as overseers of God's creation. Today's battle between environmentalists and the free marketplace is an ongoing struggle of stewardship. We continue to ignore our interdependence with nature. God created and intended a critical balance within all of creation, and theologian Jürgen Moltmann has suggested that we might do well to extend the double commandment of love to the earth: "You shall love God your Lord with all your heart, and with all your soul, and with all your strength, and your neighbors as yourself—*and this earth as yourself.*"[7]

Our ineptness and self-interest threaten the sanctity of nature. Where is the prophetic voice of the church on this matter? Discussions in the church have been limited to a small group of scholars and kindred spirits interested in a sustainable future. But to ensure peace and justice in the future we must place concern for the sanctity of nature higher on the priority list.

Human society is connected to a very complicated biological chain of life. God holds us responsible for its care and preservation. It may well be that the impending scarcity of natural resources will be the greatest barrier preventing global peace.[8] It is in our best interests to work for peace and justice by recovering the sanctity of nature. This concern will require an ecumenical group of supporters working for a common end: to establish a sustainable future for the sake of our children and grandchildren so that they might live in peace on earth.

One way to recover the sanctity of nature is to stop viewing life simply from an anthropological viewpoint. As we become more aware of and sensitive to our surroundings, we will come to appreciate better the delicate balance of nature and work for its preservation. To this end, church groups, young and old alike, should take more excursions into forests and onto mountains, with competent teachers informing us of our Creator's handiwork. More important, we must learn to curtail our consumerism and stop wasting nature's gifts. We can practice environmental tithing, reducing by one-tenth the amount of power and water we use in our homes and houses of worship.[9] Likewise, seminaries need to introduce workshops and seminars on the significance of nature. One of the more meaningful symposia I recall took place through Pittsburgh Seminary's Center for Business, Religion and the Professions as we discussed the ethics of ecology with both the chief executive officer from a major lumber company and a spokesperson for the Sierra Club, an advocacy organization for the environment. More discussion along these lines will increase our awareness that human needs are intrinsically related to nature's needs.

Guideline Three:
Identify One Another's Ultimate Hope

If peace and justice are to transpire we must have a keener understanding of one another's ultimate aspirations and hope. Our understandings of hope are largely rooted in our respective religious backgrounds. As America becomes more religiously diverse, we are no longer surprised to have Jews, Buddists, Hindus, and Muslims living in our neighborhoods. In addition, approximately a half million international students study in the United States annually at colleges, universities, and professional schools. The vast majority of these students are non-Christians. How knowledgeable are we of their faiths? For peace and justice to prevail in the future, interfaith dialogue must be encouraged. What better place for most Americans to begin than with neighbors and international students who live among us.

I suspect most of us are ignorant of the basic tenets of non-Christian religions, yet if we take the trouble to inquire, we will discover that our neighbors, like ourselves, often define their identity through religious faith. In particular, the understanding of hope is at the heart of personal belief systems. Jürgen Moltmann's book *Theology of Hope* indicates that to hope is human, but to hope in Christ is to be a Christian. Every believer has a vision for the future; to engage meaningfully with global neighbors and their faith, we will do well to understand the meaning and significance they attach to the concept of hope. Even those who claim to be nonreligious incorporate an aspect of hope in their personal vision for the future. This awareness might enable us to appreciate those with whom we converse and to have insight into their motivations and priorities. Identifying one another's ultimate hope is an important step in building peace and justice at home and abroad. Global technological and commercial ties are not sufficient to ensure peace; sooner or later we cannot escape the fact that interfaith understanding is necessary to ensure an abiding peace in the future. This is why Swiss theologian Hans Küng insists that "peace among the religions is the prerequisite for peace among the nations."[10] At the heart of this peacemaking process lies the need to appreciate one another's understanding of ultimate hope, which will uncover the forces of motivation among our non-Christian neighbors throughout our global community.

Unfortunately, hope is not universal. Many have no hope, due either to cynicism or to the marginalized condition of their lives. For the cynic, to hope in nothing can be construed as a form of liberation, freeing one from accountability. For the poor and the marginalized, the absence of hope opens the door to despair and in some cases to violence, which can be seen as a means to escape from their condition.

It is therefore essential for us as the people of God not only to witness to the hope that is within us, but also to discover the hope in other believers so that we may enhance understanding, peace, and justice. We must also reach out to those who feel hopeless, angry, and cynical to begin the difficult task of building relationships as the Holy Spirit empowers us through acts of goodwill, lest our gospel of hope seem no more than an empty gesture.

In the light of these basic guidelines, congregations may need to reevaluate their current mission programs. Most important, before beginning, we must do our homework so that we can avoid exchanging ignorance or misinformation rather than facts. We must encourage open forums at church with knowledgeable panelists to discuss the implications inherent in every peace and justice concern.

This process of learning can inform us about any number of topics: the widening gap between wealthy and poor, global warming, animal welfare, population explosion, public education, terrorism, the arms race, health coverage, AIDS, toxic waste, age and gender discrimination, corporate downsizing and the loss of loyalty, global trade and jobs, excessive consumption, welfare, illiteracy, promiscuity and abortion, safety, hunger, genetic engineering, and physician-assisted suicide.

The vital congregation will not avoid these issues; instead, it will discuss them in a manner that is fair and equitable as we pursue the truth in Christ and the desire to be faithful to each person's dignity and destiny. Reviving the church calls for every congregation to be involved as a learning community, translating its knowledge into deeds that promote peace and justice.

Discussion Starter

Are peace and justice issues doomed to divide us? What steps would you take to work for the church's unity without neglecting peace and justice concerns?

Chapter Ten

Be People of Trust

Can the Clergy Be Trusted?

We live in an age of suspicion and distrust. Society's expectations of professionals and institutions are lower than ever. Why have we lost this trust among ourselves? Why have we become a culture of distrust?

According to public policy specialist Darwell West of Brown University, "the rising level of mistrust is the most profound change in public opinion over the last three decades. If you go back to the 1950s, about 70% trusted the government in Washington to do the right thing. Today about 70% mistrust the government. There is no other change that is that dramatic."[1] We have moved from the 1960s slogan "Don't trust anyone over thirty" to the present temperament of 1990s:— "Don't trust *anyone.*"

Within this context some people view former television news anchor Walter Cronkite as the most trusted American living today, prompting Cronkite himself to wonder, "Why should a TV personality be deemed most trustworthy?"[2] Why indeed? Clergy, unfortunately, are no longer regarded as the most trusted professionals in America. Why has the public, and that includes parishioners, become so cynical that seemingly all leaders, including the clergy, are not trusted? Some measure of distrust may be an important element in everyone's survival kit. Surely, anyone who has been the victim of professional malpractice, a bad business deal, or a poorly designed product is reluctant to trust anything or anyone without reservation. A reasonable level of suspicion is essential. Yet we know that we cannot exist meaningfully or help one another without trust. This is especially true for the religious leader who cannot practice ministry effectively without being trusted by the congregation and community. To what extent has this loss of trust, more than any other single factor, contributed to the church's decline and the mounting suspicion within our church structures today?

I suspect no survey will ever reliably tell us what happened to create "church dropouts" and an even larger number who are simply indifferent or suspicious of the church today. Restoring credibility is never an easy task, and there are no shortcuts. A top priority for ministry today is to be engaged in trust building, if our message of hope in Christ is to be heard and our efforts at evangelism are to have enduring significance.

For church renewal to go forward, trust building must be paramount on the church's agenda and among its leadership. We can take action to restore trust by practicing the following:

1. We must be accepting of others. We must see promise and potential even in situations others overlook. We need to relate to the marginal and questionable in our society with forgiving love that disarms their suspicions and provides hope beyond their cynicism.

2. We must be accessible to youth as well as to adults. Youth can often distinguish authenticity from insincerity. We need to invite everyone to enjoy the church's hospitality. We must practice an open door policy no matter how busy we are; we must keep our agenda flexible. We cannot operate with a time clock mentality; we need to expect more than a forty-hour week, we must willingly accept interruptions.

3. We must have the courage to express ourselves with candor and clarity. We must also know how to live with ambiguity as we instruct followers to accept mystery until their comprehension can catch up with their experience.

4. We must teach and speak with humility and competence.

We must master our materials and understand human nature; we must be able to present a fresh angle on issues, teaching creatively and addressing matters that count. In our encounters with others, we must show ourselves to be outstanding teachers who are able to listen and be corrected at times as well.

5. We must make every effort to communicate concretely through stories and deeds. We must seek to capture the imagination of listeners, inviting them to interact in lively dialogue with us.

6. We must practice silence when needed. We need to maintain confidentiality on delicate issues and practice sensitivity appropriately in various contexts.

7. We must always maintain a caring spirit, in spite of personal stress. Our circle of concern must be larger than our friends and enemies expect. Our acts of caring can lead to disagreements among followers, while at the same time challenging the establishment. Our stance on issues may be disliked by many in power while loved by outcasts. In all circumstances, let us ask God for Solomon's wisdom, namely, the gift of hindsight before the event, listening with the heart as well as the head.

8. We must be strategic planners who intentionally prepare our people for the kingdom of God. We must carefully mentor future leaders. We need to provide the framework for future ministry with an emphasis on forgiving love, repentance, and integrity, teaching ourselves to be dependent upon a gracious God who accepts us in spite of ourselves.

9. Finally, we gain trust by living a life with purpose. Our own leadership must have a clear sense of direction, a desire to do justice, show mercy, and practice humility before God and neighbor (Micah 6:8). We must not trade core convictions for shallow compromises. We ought to move with a strong sense of mission. We must faithfully follow the will of God, whatever the cost. With God's help, we can become people of God worthy of trust, effectively confronting the challenges of today and tomorrow.[3]

An Exercise in Trust Building:
The Shoemaker Roundtable

Not only is trust in the clergy needed, but also trust within the membership as well. The people of God, clergy and laity as a leadership team, must *be* people of trust, mutually accountable and biblically informed as all move to deepen their trust in God. Then and only then can we build the foundation for a visionary church whose witness is vitally demonstrated daily within and without its walls.

It is true that the church matters, that theology matters and that Jesus matters, but let's not forget that all our declarations are endangered when we overlook the important factor that character matters. Trust building among the people of God is essential if we wish the church to be characterized as a fellowship of Christians who enjoy genuine trust among themselves. What a powerful example for a society immersed in suspicion and distrust! Unfortunately, the church too often mirrors society rather than being an alternative model that exemplifies a higher quality of life—an accepting and forgiving fellowship that places ultimate trust in God.

Not long ago, Pittsburgh Seminary sponsored the G. Albert Shoemaker Roundtable conference on the church's mission for the future. The gathering to a large extent was an exercise in trust building among the forty participants—clergy, scholars, lay leaders, and denominational executives in the Presbyterian Church (U.S.A.).

Participants had expressed through a questionnaire prior to the conference their confusion over the church's raison d'etre. Discussion began around some of the problems and paradoxes facing the church today: pragmatic marketing vs. doing God's work; "if we follow Jesus, numbers don't matter"; give them what they want vs. give them what they need; strategy vs. leadership; getting people to church vs. getting people on the path; following successful models vs. being yourself; having integrity; extroverted community building vs. introspective; getting in touch with yourself; architectural design is important vs. only the spirit is important; and centralized governance vs. decentralized governance.

The issue that arose first was whether the conference group itself was a community. The answer was clear—there existed suspicion and mistrust in our midst. As the discussion moved tentatively from mistrust to candor over disagreements, participants began to experience authentic dialogue. Furthermore, they affirmed qualities of the Presbyterian Church that create a spirit of community: service and missionary work with people in need, democratic decision making, equality between the sexes with women in prominent roles.

As the conference came to an end, the group sensed a moment of divine convergence driven by a common vision and a willingness to be a community in mission to further common goals. In that moment, they found what it means to be a community of God in the making, and they articulated the following mission statement:

> Believing that God is redeeming the world through Jesus Christ, we are forgiven and called to discipleship. Seeking to respond to God, we work to transform society in the lives of individuals. Being drawn by the power of the Holy Spirit, we nurture communities of faith that glorify God and engage in ministries of peace and justice.

For a brief time, the group was able to envision what it meant to be the community of God, working for wholeness that incorporates diversity, practicing forgiveness and acceptance toward one another, recognizing and naming shared values, and, most important, wanting to work together toward a common purpose. This experience supports what John W. Gardner, founder of Common Cause, has observed:

> Individuals have a role in the continuous rebuilding of the value of framework and the best thing that they can do is not to preach values but to exemplify them. Teach the truth by living it. All of us celebrate our values and our behavior.

It is the universal ministry. The way we act and conduct our lives is saying something to others—perhaps something reprehensible, perhaps something encouraging.[4]

The participants of the Shoemaker Roundtable experienced in the short time together a growing sense of caring, trust, and teamwork as they learned to listen with empathy rather than expound in a monologue fashion. At the same time they engaged and affirmed one another through their encounters and fellowship at the conference. They acted as the people of God who saw themselves as the body of Christ. They realized that no one can ever take the church's future and mission for granted. The need to reform ourselves calls for constant vigilance according to scripture and the Spirit's leading. The group's sights were lifted, they desired to become the community of God in the making, a gathering of believers in a place it is safe to raise doubts, express feelings, and explore a wide range of ideas based on our freedom and commitment in Christ.

The Congregation That Trusts
Together Is in Mission Together

Perhaps the most effective and productive way to become people of trust is to develop a mission outlook as a congregation to the surrounding world, to be the people of God in action together. As we work together in service projects and mission programs, we will learn to build trust and respect for one another's talents and dedication. Gardner is right—the world wants to hear our preaching through our lives and deeds. Do we exemplify what we preach, teach, and celebrate sacramentally?

It has been my experience that both pastors and parishioners are searching for their dream church, the church they always wanted to be active in but could not find. A "shopping mall mentality" in spiritual matters seems to be the prevailing mood. Some are even building the "virtual church" on their computer screens and wish it could be substituted for the real thing that eludes them. We need to shift from computer games to the actualities confronting today's believer, beginning with the realization that there is no "Christian America." This fact is a wake-up call that many congregations refuse to heed. To be a visionary and vital church in tomorrow's world is to grasp the fact that we are living in a post-Christian society. If in our moments of clarity we know this is true, why do we persist in holding on to outdated perceptions and inflated numerical data, denying the reality of our minority status in a secularized society?[5]

In recent times we have witnessed the marginalization of Christian commitment within our ranks; even civil religion has lost its societal respectability. Stephen Carter of Yale University Law School claims we live essentially in a "culture of disbelief." The majority of Americans continue to believe in a generic God, a divine someone, who is there on a stand-by basis whenever there is an emergency in their lives. Most Americans shy away from any serious commitment that might cost something. Afraid of fanaticism or fundamentalism, most believers have a nominal faith as the careful prudent course to follow in life.

To meet this challenge of growing indifference, we must discipline ourselves to become a resourceful minority willing to commit ourselves to the sake of Christ. We admire the stories of Dietrich Bonhoeffer, Mother Teresa, and Desmond Tutu, but most of us haven't the desire or the will to follow their example. At the same time, we know it is a difficult world, and belief in a generic God simply will not be enough to nourish us. We must be more focused in our faith, fed with the biblical manna to sustain and motivate us. As we practice our message of healing forgiveness through Christ, Christians *can* make a difference in a society of broken relationships.

However, let's be realistic; the odds are against us. The world is not receptive to our message of forgiveness. We are strangers to peace and show a tendency to hate and violence.

The bombing in Oklahoma City is still burning in our memories. Our capacity for wrongdoing shocks us. We think more highly of ourselves than the evidence justifies. We are more preoccupied with the question "why do bad things happen to good people?" than "why do good people do bad things?" We have lost the underlying sacredness and significance of Christmas and Easter.

As people of God, we need to comprehend the situation confronting us. Only then can we strategize as a determined minority to proclaim the message entrusted to us. If only we could truly envision (through our computer screens or otherwise) what we can become, we would reenergize ourselves and be more willing to change, to take the necessary risk required of us. We need to see, as if for the first time, the beauty of a society where love, justice, and peace prevail. We need to envision the reign of God as the last great hope to reidentify the divine image tarnished in us and rediscover the common ground of our humanity as witnessed in our Lord's earthly ministry.

We need to recapture the intensity of our "first love" for God, whom we have come to trust through Christ. Loving God in Jesus Christ helps us break out of countless stereotypes—ethnic, economic, racial, gender, or whatever—that prevent us from building a bonding community. In Christ, says the apostle Paul, there is no Jew or Greek, no rich or poor, no slave or free, no woman or man; we are all one, mutually called upon to respect and uphold God's image in one another (Gal. 3:28).

Unfortunately, the majority within our culture is influenced by other temporal realities: power, money, and status. As a global minority we must transcend these penultimate realities. We must make God the overriding influence is our lives. Yet, it seems the vast majority of the human race finds it difficult to hear the still small voice of God's Spirit—our culture is too noisy and our lives too busy. Prayer too has become difficult, and when we do pray, it tends too often to be self-serving and self-centered. It seems we have no time to practice God's presence; we are more interested in keeping in step with our surrounding culture. The challenge before us is so great! To be counted among the company of the committed, God's minority, is the distinct call of Christian discipleship today.

We must become more intentional, more assertive about our central mission in life. We need to recover again the missionary nature of the church, proclaiming without apology the good news of God's forgiveness in Christ and its healing powers within our scared and suspicious world. Kennon L. Callahan of the National Institute for Church Planning and Consultation makes the prophetic observation:

> The day of the professional minister is over, the day of the missionary pastor has come. . . . The day of the church culture is over, the day of the mission field has come. . . . The day of the local church is over, the day of the mission outpost has come.[6]

As a committed minority, we need to regain the missionary spirit of the apostle Paul, who took the challenge of John 3:16 to heart, reaching out to the world. Let's not get caught in the false debate between church growth and being faithful. The truth is that we are neither growing nor being faithful today. When we are truly faithful, we will be a growing church. Any growth not rooted in faithfulness to Christ will not last.

Our hope is to be a faithful minority disciplined in mind, heart, and soul, led by the Holy Spirit to let the church be the church. Then and only then can the church be revived. For now, we are called to be the salt of the earth, the mustard seed that grows, the yeast that multiplies, and the light that illuminates the darkness. And with discipline, we will emerge as the body of Christ empowered by the pioneer and perfecter of our faith.

Discussion Starter

Is there anyone you can trust? Describe the qualities of trust in that relationship. What lesson does it hold for the church? If you are unable to trust, why is this so?

Becoming the Church for the Next Century

This is an exciting time for the people of God to be in ministry. We are living between old wineskins and new ones. We are at a crossroads, deciding whether to fuss further with patching old wineskins or discard them for the new.

The Old or the New?

For many, these new wineskins are seen in the outreach of parachurch ministries, such as Promise Keepers, Navigators, Young Life, Campus Crusade for Christ, and Inter-Varsity Christian Fellowship. Others find new wineskins in the much publicized megachurches, often referred to as full-service churches.

Perhaps the best known of these churches is the Willow Creek Church in Barrington, Illinois, where more than 20,000 people regularly attend services. A budget of fifteen million dollars includes the salaries of the church's 192 full-time employees. There are approximately four hundred megachurches in the United States today, and the Willow Creek Association has been formed with 1,400 churches in North America to teach and promote the "Willow Creek principles" in their own neighborhoods and regions. According to a 1996 article in the *Atlantic Monthly,* "Half of all church-going Americans . . . are attending only 12 percent of the nation's 400,000 churches. To look at it in another way, half of American Protestant churches have fewer than seventy-five congregants."[1]

We do not know what the church will be like in 2050, but

we need to ask whether the "brand name" mainline denominations—Methodist, Reformed, Episcopal, Lutheran, American Baptist, United Church of Christ, Disciples of Christ, and Presbyterian—will be but a remnant of themselves. The present decline casts a doubtful future for denominations, and, I suspect, creates anxiety for younger seminarians who represent these denominations.

We need leadership with the courage, intelligence, and commitment to Christ and to the church to creatively lead us to the cutting edge of mission in the next century. We seek future leaders among the clergy and the laity who have a keen desire to make a difference; not simply institutional maintenance keepers, but those who have the capacity to consider and act on what is at stake—the demise or revitalization of our ecclesial institutions.

Many questions bear down upon us. Is the core mission of the church worth preserving? What "holy gamble" should these mainline churches make with their limited resources if they wish to be significant players in the next century? Are we defending the status quo out of fear of the unknown? What is the right thing to do? Will we go on trying to do things right, but fail to do the right thing?

The Reality of Change

How inviting will our houses of worship be for those born after 1990 who may or may not wish to identify with the Christian church in the next century? We cannot take the next generation or two for granted; we ought to have learned that lesson from the generation of baby boomers and baby busters, some of whom find the megachurches appealing. To what extent is theological education sensitive to the stresses confronting local churches? Are we in the seminaries willing to participate meaningfully and relevantly in educating leadership for the church in the next century? Or is the present curriculum in our seminaries simply a projection of faculty interests and needs? What overriding bias rules among theological faculties today, to stick with old wineskins or begin to stitch new ones? Seminary communities are not safe havens from the turmoil and confusion felt at the grassroots; seminaries and churches are connected institutions that need to support and assist one another in articulating the gospel message.

Others of us might sigh with relief that we will not be around in 2050; perhaps we can hold out, grasping for that invisible contract we signed where the church promised not to abandon us if we were faithful in upholding our end of the bargain, regardless of how many worldly changes there are. There is no doubt we will need a measure of stability in our lives, and isn't this the expected role of the church? Yet none of us can escape the reality of change; even death is a changing event that awaits each of us. The big question is whether churches and related institutions can master dynamic continuity while sailing on stormy seas of change.

The only way to address change is to face it in a reforming spirit, to be willing to be led by the winds of the Spirit into unknown territory, to take a risk, driven by an abiding vision to realize the kingdom of God. We cannot afford to harbor illusions that churches or seminaries are bastions of safety against forces of change. To maintain such an attitude is to become obsolete. In this information and learning age, as never before, we need to justify our actions not only to ourselves but to a spiritually starved society that craves spirituality largely without the aid of the church.

Developing a New Mindset

Perhaps we should acquire a mindset that views all existing churches (of whatever size) as new church developments. How then would we go about establishing an "ideal church" for the next century that is theologically and biblically sound, caring and nurturing, socially relevant and electronically connected? To imagine each of our existing churches (in spite of present circumstances and restrictions) as new church developments might provide a fresh angle of vision. Might each new church development see itself first and foremost as a Christian witness in a pluralistic neighborhood whose goal is to interest the unchurched, many of whom are no doubt indifferent or suspicious of the church, having largely dismissed its relevance in their youth? Some will elect to be part of a new church development, excited to build a model of what the church could be. It is precisely this new church mentality that we need to adopt if we are to transcend the restricting circumstances choking us in our present situations. Perhaps by this means of planning for the future we may find a more satisfactory approach in which to envision the church as it ought to be if it is to flourish and educate effectively in the next century. This way of thinking may be a jump start, liberating us from present inertia and feelings of despair.

The same is true for us in seminary education. Perhaps we ought to engage ourselves in designing a new seminary for the next century in spite of the given constraints each school faces. For many schools, this may be a clarion call for zero-based curriculum planning, where every course and teaching method would need to be justified. The struggle over turf would also be discussed openly among colleagues. It is my hope that this could take place in an atmosphere of some security with a growing appreciation and trust for one another, a necessary premise for genuine communication in any organization. Seminaries could model for the churches the dialogical attitude needed in facing change and the critical issues that will surface and have already into the next century. We need to be clear why we exist and for what we stand, but this does not mean that we need to be wedded to the old and traditional in carrying out our mission. We need to become shepherds of dynamic continuity as we transfer the core of our beliefs and values into new wineskins that have not yet been stitched together, seeking to preserve the best of our proud heritage and with humility and hope looking to the future.

The planning process for envisioning the "ideal church" and the "ideal seminary" must incorporate synthetic, or systemic, thinking. Most of our thinking process is primarily preoccupied with analysis. The analytical approach points us to structures and asks, how does it work? The analytical method breaks the whole down into minute parts for examination and change to improve efficiency. It enables us to do things right.

However, doing things right may be the wrong approach! That may sound paradoxical. Yet, I am afraid that is what has happened in reorganizing attempts (for instance, in the Presbyterian Church [U.S.A.]) that I have witnessed since 1958 when I was ordained. I suspect the same might be said of reorganizing efforts in other mainline denominations. We have been too analytical! The analytic approach is geared to research and solving a problem, examining and correcting the parts that lead to the whole. Analytical thinking is detail oriented, but for the most part it does not envision adequately the big picture.

On the other hand, synthetic or systemic thinking is occupied with function rather than structure. It is concerned with dissolving messes. Instead of asking how something works, synthetic thinking is concerned with function, asking, what is the role? Synthetic thinking seeks understanding rather than knowledge. It aims for effectiveness, for doing the right thing rather than doing things right. It is primarily design oriented rather than detail oriented. It looks to the whole (the ideal church or seminary) and then to the appropriation of necessary parts that would enable us to function at our best. Synthetic thinking, for instance, would beckon us to envision the kingdom of God and then to proceed toward that end under the Spirit's guidance.

I was introduced to this way of thinking as a participant at an invitational workshop sponsored by the Tallberg Foundation under the theme "Preparing for the 21st Century: Leadership in an Age of Learning." Russell L. Ackoff of the University of Pennsylvania stimulated us to think beyond the use of analytical skills, to employ a systems approach as we prepare ourselves for challenges of the next century.[2] You might wish to examine this method as discussed in Peter M. Senge's book, *The Fifth Discipline: The Art and Practice of the Organization*, where the emphasis is also upon systems or synthetic thinking.

The challenge I received from the Tallberg workshop can be summed up in this quote from Albert Einstein: "We cannot solve the problems we have created with the same thinking that created them." We might modify his quote slightly and say for our purposes, "We are unable to solve the problems we have created with the same theologizing and church practices that have created them."

Recently, a mainline pastor shared with me his concerns about ministry. He admitted that he could not wait to retire. "Why?" I asked. "You are only fifty years old and have at least fifteen years of active ministry before you." He replied, "I'm not alone in my feelings; there are a number of my colleagues who feel the same way. We don't want to 'rock the boat' any longer, the ship is clearly too fragile. At the same time, I no longer feel I can exercise my freedom in Christ before the congregation. I find myself simply offering churchgoers what they want to hear and that keeps me out of trouble."

How would you respond to this pastor's fatigue and loss of purpose? He was expressing frustration and despair; his personal unwritten contract for ministry as he envisioned it was to bring prophetic renewal to the church. However, he is finding the old wineskin inadequate and beyond repair, and yet is afraid to use a new one. He finds himself increasingly lonely in a cultural wasteland where street signs are torn down and where stoplights are not longer dependable; the present flow of traffic and noise in and out of the church no longer makes sense to him. The paradigm has shifted for him; unfortunately, he feels nostalgia for an earlier context and is still grasping tightly in his hand an invisible contract he made when he accepted his call to ministry.

How many parishioners are there in the pews today who have similar feelings and have dropped out or have taken early retirement from church life for a number of personal reasons? An active churchwoman told me recently that she took a "sabbatical" from church for several months and was surprised to find that she did not miss it. Is she on the way to becoming another church drop out? My hope is that neither this pastor nor parishioner will give up on the church, but be reenergized by discovering and practicing a systemic way of thinking and thereby implement steps toward an ideal church. Working in small increments, we can behold in time something new and exciting formed by the grace of God and through the guidance of the Spirit. As we work then to fulfill the ideal, we can celebrate each step of progress to the glory of God. Don't for a moment think that this synthetic process is easy; it takes hard work and constant empowerment through prayer.

Toward the Community of God

I believe we can enter a "new reformation" for denominations if we are willing to shed old wineskins for new ones that we presently cannot envision clearly.[3] But first we must have a consenting will to work toward an ideal institution (church and seminary) that will take us beyond our fragmented theologies and present skirmishes. We need to be liberated to think more holistically and synthetically. We need to shift from analytical thinking to synthetic approaches envisioning the ideal church and the ideal seminary for the next century. There must be a will on our part to take the risk, individually and collectively, and then to move out by means of dialogue and experimentation to incorporate the characteristics that go into a community that resembles the kingdom of God. Our task, in a spirit of discipleship and discipline, is to turn a church or seminary into a vibrant community of God motivated by divine love and forgiveness in Christ, enabling us to practice joyful openness with one another. More specifically, we need to promote the incarnate characteristics of the community of God in the following ways:

1. We must endeavor to be the community of wholeness that incorporates diversity. A community of diversity has greater opportunity to accept and renew itself in a swiftly changing world. Finding wholeness and coherence within our diversity will overcome fragmentation not only in our churches, but in our cities and neighborhoods as well. The church must become the model of community among communities to make wholeness credible. There is no doubt that a new church development mentality must be our outlook. The sooner we engage in this task, the sooner we will find ourselves doing the right thing as we enter a new millennium.

2. We need to become the community of forgiveness and acceptance. Who of us is without sin? Perhaps we ought to take a clue from the twelve-step organizations, and be bonded at first through our confessions and struggles, but then push on for a deeper unity through Christ as we become biblically literate with the sacramental symbols and stories of scripture to inspire us.

3. We must become the community of shared values. Churches need to be defined by the values they are willing to defend, and believers must know that the society and media will be there to test our sincerity. Are we then truly willing to stand up for what we believe amid the ambiguities in our society?[4]

4. We must become the community of caring, trust, and teamwork. Reality resides in relationships; we need to nurture authentic relations with one another. This does not mean we need to abolish conflict, but must work toward constructive outcomes from our disagreements.

5. We must become the community of listening as we seek to communicate with one another. We will discover, if we have not already, that a common language helps. Speaking English, however, does not mean necessarily that we are speaking a common language. It goes far deeper than that! We must understand and appreciate one another's passions and life histories if we are to truly communicate.

6. We must become the community of engagement and participation. Everyone is important and has a role to play. Positive involvement enhances self-esteem and a sense of belonging to the community.

7. We must become the community of affirmation. By this means we can empower one another. A word of encouragement and an honest compliment can go far in lifting spirits to do our task.

8. We must be the community of fun and celebration. Everyone works together better when we can play and enjoy one another's company. There is too little fun and play presently in our church and seminary life to really contribute to fellowship and a sense of togetherness. Most of us are too busy, and perhaps we take ourselves too seriously. Lightening up is important in relating successfully to one another.

9. We need to be the community that embraces all ages; where youth are welcome and the elderly are embraced. These two groups have been neglected—greater investment is required from the younger adult members of the community. Parachurch organizations are replacing the vacuum felt within the church. Seminaries need to direct their attention to offering programs and nurturing leadership for all ages.

10. We need to be the community that looks beyond itself. A church community must engage in networking with a wide range of organizations, never losing sight of our own unique mission and purpose in society. Creative alliances will be needed more than ever in the next century.

11. We must be the community that never takes its own mission and direction for granted. We must be open to the future while constantly evaluating our current activities. In our witness before the surrounding society, we must demonstrate a sense of divine connectedness, never forgetting who we are and whose will we seek to honor.

12. In this incomplete listing of characteristics of the community of God in the making, we need to become a safe place where our thoughts, doubts, and feelings can be expressed. We

must uphold one another in prayer as we take mutual responsibility for each person's daily walk in faith.

The church in the next century will take bold steps to envision the kingdom of God in its midst, discovering in the process that this is God's will for the church. We are called to be the community of love, nurtured by the triune God whose essence is the embodiment of love within a divine community. Reaching the kingdom of God, our hope and destiny, calls for nothing less than entering this community of God, a perfect fellowship of oneness, more beautiful than we can ever imagine (see John 17). Let us dare to discard old wineskins, discovering and embracing new ones to lead us onward to the promised kingdom of God as we become the church for the next century.

"Veni, Creator Spiritus," Come, Creator Spirit.

NOTES

Introduction

1. This is the basic point made by John N. Leith in his recent book, *Crisis in the Church: The Plight of Theological Education* (Louisville, Ky: Westminster John Knox Press, 1997).
2. Roger Fisher and William Ury have coauthored a useful volume entitled, *Getting to Yes: Negotiating Agreement without Giving In* (Boston: Houghton Mifflin, 1981). Ury also has a more recent book, *Getting Past No: Negotiating Your Way from Confrontation to Cooperation* (New York: Bantam Books, 1993). Many conflicts within congregations could be helped by practicing the insights outlined in these books.
3. See Carnegie Samuel Calian, *Theology without Boundaries: Encounters of Eastern Orthodoxy and Western Traditions* (Louisville, Ky.: Westminster/John Knox Press, 1992).
4. Cited in Rushworth M. Kidder, *Shared Values for a Troubled World: Conversations with Men and Women of Conscience* (San Francisco: Jossey-Bass, 1994), 198.
5. Ibid.
6. Ibid. I had the good fortune to meet Professor Gardner in the summer of 1995 when I was a visiting scholar at Stanford University. I am grateful to him and many of the faculty members at Stanford's Graduate School of Business for sharing their insights on the dynamics of organizational life in the business world. Two books on organizational life I recommend are James C. Collins and Jerry I. Porras, *Built to Last: Successful Habits of Visionary Companies* (San Francisco: HarperSanFrancisco, 1994), and Robert Kelley, *The Power of Followership* (New York: Doubleday, 1992). See also Carnegie Samuel Calian, *Where's the Passion for Excellence in the Church?* (Wilton, Conn.: Morehouse-Barlow, 1989).

Chapter 1

1. Jim Taylor, "If God Got Voice-Mail," *Perspectives: A Journal of Reformed Thought* (May 1997): 9.
2. Cited in *Presbyterians Today* (July/August 1997): 24.
3. Margo G. Houts, "Is God Also Our Mother?" *Perspectives: A Journal of Reformed Thought* (June/July 1997): 7.
4. For a discussion on Eastern and Western methods for theologizing

see Vladimir Lossky, *The Mystical Theology of the Eastern Church* (Oxford: James Clarke & Co., 1957) and Carnegie Samuel Calian, *Icon and Pulpit: The Protestant-Orthodox Encounter* (Philadelphia: Westminster Press, 1968).

5. Houts, "Is God Also Our Mother?" 12.
6. "A Brief Statement of Faith," *The Book of Confessions,* Presbyterian Church (U.S.A), 10.11. Published by The Office of the General Assembly, 1991.
7. Ibid., 10.3.
8. Ibid., 10.5.

Chapter 2

1. A book of studies made for the National Institute of Literacy (800 Connecticut Avenue, NW, Suite 200, Washington, DC). Also see *One World* (December 1991): 16–17.
2. The formation of these questions is attributed to the German philosopher Immanuel Kant (1724–1804).
3. If you wish to pursue a fuller discussion, see my book, *Theology without Boundaries: Encounters of Eastern Orthodoxy and Western Tradition* (Louisville, Ky.: Westminster/John Knox Press, 1992), 45–50. Much of the discussion today stimulated by the work of the Jesus Seminar is in actuality an underlying quest for an authoritative interpretation of scripture.
4. See James A. Sanders, "The Bible as Canon," *Christian Century* (December 2, 1981): 1250–55. See also Peter J. Gomes, *The Good Book: Reading the Bible with Mind and Heart* (New York: William Morrow & Co., 1996).
5. William C. Placher, "Is the Bible True?" *Christian Century* (October 11, 1995): 924–28. See also Richard B. Hays, "Salvation by Trust? Reading the Bible Faithfully," *Christian Century* (February 26, 1997): 218–23.
6. Ibid.

Chapter 3

1. See, for example, J. Walker Smith and Ann Clurman, *Rocking the Ages: The Yankelovich Report on Generational Marketing* (New York: Harper Business, 1997), 292–305.
2. For a fuller discussion of this needed partnership see C. S. Calian, *Today's Pastor in Tomorrow's World,* rev. ed. (Philadelphia: Westminster Press, 1989).
3. Petru Dumitriu, *To the Unknown God* (New York: Seabury Press, 1982), 191. Dumitriu was converted from Marxism.
4. Other Swiss Reformers were Heinrich Bullinger (1404–1475) of Zurich, John Oecolampadius (1482–1531) of Basel, Berchtold

Haller (1492–1536) of Berne, and Guillaume Farel (1489–1565) of Neuchâtel.

5. An interview with Lewis Dupree under the title, "Seeking Christian Interiority," *Christian Century* (July 16–23, 1997): 654.

Chapter 4

1. Cited in Dean Merrill, "How a Lieutenant in the Moral Majority Rediscovered the Power of the Local Church," *Christianity Today* (August 11, 1997): 29.

2. For a fuller discussion on evangel and evangelism, see my book, *Grace, Guts and Goods: How to Stay Christian in an Affluent Society* (Nashville: Thomas Nelson, 1971), especially pp. 57–65. See also the booklet by Hugh B. Berry, *Being a Welcoming Congregation,* published by the Presbyterian Church (U.S.A.), 1996.

3. See the discussion of Willow Creek's ministry in Katrina Burger, "Jesus Christ.com," *Forbes* (May 5, 1997): 76–81. See also David S. Leucke, "Is Willow Creek the Way of the Future?" and James L. Kidd, "Megachurch Method," *Christian Century* (May 14, 1997): 479–85.

Chapter 5

1. Eugene H. Peterson, *The Message: New Testament with Psalms and Proverbs* (Colorado Springs: Navpress, 1993), 646–47.

2. Ibid., 647.

3. See John Calvin, *Institutes of the Christian Religion,* ed. John T. McNeill, Library of Christian Classics, Vol. XX and XXI (Philadelphia: Westminster Press, 1960). This memorable work is a classic expression of the Christian faith according to the Reformed tradition.

4. Abraham Joshua Heschel, *Man's Quest for God: Studies in Prayer and Symbolism* (New York: Scribner, 1954), 62.

5. William James, *The Varieties of Religious Experience* (Cambridge: Harvard University Press, 1985), 365.

6. St. Augustine, *The Confessions of St. Augustine,* trans. Hal M. Helms (Orleans, Mass.: Paraclete Press, 1986), 1.1.1.

7. Cited in Karl Barth, *Prayer* (Philadelphia: Westminster Press, 1962), 9–10.

8. William Easum, *Dancing with Dinosaurs: Ministry in a Hostile and Hurting World* (Nashville: Abingdon Press, 1993), 13–14.

9. Ibid.

10. Ronald Goetz, "On Petitionary Prayer: Pleading with the Unjust Judge," *Christian Century* (January 1997): 97. See this issue also for responses to Goetz's article.

11. Taken from a church newsletter, *The Correspondent* (August

1997), published by the Community of Reconciliation in Pittsburgh.

Chapter 6
1. Margot Hornblower, "Great Xpectations," *Time* (June 9, 1997): 60.
2. Ibid.
3. Melinda Beck, "Next Population Bulge Shows Its Might," *Wall Street Journal* (February 3, 1997).
4. Claudia Wallis, "Faith and Healing," *Time* (June 14, 1996): 59–68, and also reported in the *Ecumenical News International Bulletin* (July 9, 1996): 8–9.
5. Peter L. Benson, Dorothy Williams, Carolyn H. Eklin, and David Schuller, "Effective Christian Education: A National Study of Protestant Congregations" (Minneapolis: Search Institute, 1990): 2.

Chapter 7
1. See his book, *Reclaiming the Church: Where the Mainline Church Went Wrong and What to Do about It* (Louisville, Ky.: Westminster John Knox Press, 1997).
2. Marilee Monger Scroggs, "Making a Difference—Fourth Presbyterian Church of Chicago," in *American Congregation*, vol. 1, ed. James P. Wind and James W. Lewis (Chicago: University of Chicago Press, 1994), 508. See also John Buchanan, *Being Church, Becoming Community* (Louisville, Ky.: Westminster John Knox Press, 1996).
3. Robert Kelley, *The Power of Followership* (New York: Doubleday, 1992), 7–8.
4. Ibid., 42.
5. Ibid., 46.
6. I am glad to report that an anonymous donor recently caught that vision on behalf of our school. We inaugurated on November 12, 1997, the Robert H. Meneilly Chair of Leadership and Ministry at Pittsburgh Theological Seminary.

Chapter 8
1. Søren Kierkegaard, *Works of Love: Some Christian Reflections in the Form of Discourses* (New Jersey: Princeton University Press, 1995), 294–5.
2. Paul Lehmann, *Forgiveness: Decisive Issue in Protestant Thought* (New York: Harper & Brothers, 1940), 140.

3. H. R. Mackintosh, *The Christian Experience of Forgiveness* (London: Nisbet & Co., 1927), 183.
4. Robert D. Brinsmead, "The Need for a Covenantal Framework," *Verdict* (November 1979), 25.
5. See, for example, Bushnell, Horace, *The Vicarious Sacrifice* (1866) and *Forgiveness and Law* (New York: Scribners, 1874); Mackintosh, *The Christian Experience of Forgiveness* (1927); Donald Baillie, *God Was in Christ* (New York: Scribners, 1948); Leonard Hodgson, *The Doctrine of the Atonement* (London: Nisbet 1951).
6. The literature has multiplied in recent years. See, for example, Fisher Humphreys, *The Death of Christ* (Nashville: Broadman, 1978); Rachel Henderlite, *Forgiveness and Hope* (Richmond: John Knox Press, 1962); James G. Emerson Jr., *The Dynamics of Forgiveness* (Philadelphia: Westminster Press, 1964); William Klassen, *The Forgiving Community* (Philadelphia: Westminster Press, 1966); Dorothee Soelle, *Suffering* (Philadelphia: Fortress Press, 1975); Doris Donnelly, *Learning to Forgive* (New York: Macmillan, 1979), Carl Reinhold Brakenhielm, *Forgiveness* (Minneapolis: Fortress Press, 1993); J. G. Haber, *Forgiveness* (Baltimore: Rowman & Littlefield, 1991), L. Gregory Jones, *Embodying Forgiveness: A Theological Analysis* (Grand Rapids: Wm. B. Eerdmans Publishing Co., 1995); and also Jones's chapter on "Forgiveness" in *Practicing Our Faith: A Way of Life for a Searching People*, ed. Dorothy C. Bass (San Francisco: Jossey-Bass, 1997).
7. For a fuller discussion of this aspect, see my book, *For All Your Seasons: Biblical Direction through Life's Passages* (Atlanta: John Knox Press, 1979), 40–43. See also Lewis B. Smedes, *Forgive and Forget: Healing the Hurts We Don't Deserve* (New York: Harper & Row, 1984).
8. Paul Tillich, *The New Being* (New York: Charles Scribner's Sons, 1955), 13. See also Daniel Day Williams, "Paul Tillich's Doctrine of Forgiveness," *Pastoral Psychology* 19, no. 181 (February 1968): 17–21. See also the articles on forgiveness in *Parabola* (fall 1987). We plan to explore further this relationship between forgiveness and healing at our recently established Carter Consortium on Faith and Health to be jointly sponsored by Pittsburgh Seminary and the Graduate School of Public Health at the University of Pittsburgh.
9. Langdon Gilkey, *Naming the Whirlwind* (Indianapolis: Bobbs-Merrill Co., 1969), 407.
10. Joseph Haroutunian, "Grace and Freedom Reconsidered," *Journal of Religion* 40 (1960): 73.

11. Kenneth L. Woodward, "Religion: To Forgive Is Human, Too," *Newsweek* (January 16, 1995): 62.

Chapter 9

1. Donald W. Shriver Jr., *An Ethic for Enemies: Forgiveness in Politics* (New York: Oxford University Press, 1995), 230.
2. Ibid., 231.
3. Ibid.
4. This insight was made by Michael Maccoby, psychotherapist and author, in an unpublished paper we jointly wrote entitled, "Vision, Religion and the Communitarian Spirit."
5. Shriver, *An Ethic for Enemies*, 232.
6. "American Opinion," *Wall Street Journal* (December 13, 1996), R4.
7. Jürgen Moltmann, *The Source of Life: The Holy Spirit and the Theology of Life* (Minneapolis: Fortress Press, 1997), 49.
8. See Larry L. Rasmussen, *Earth Community, Earth Ethics* (Maryknoll, N.Y.: Orbis Books, 1996); and Sallie McFague, *The Body of Christ: An Ecological Theology* (Minneapolis: Fortress Press, 1993).
9. See Sharon Daloz Parks, "Household Economics," in *Practicing our Faith*, ed. Dorothy C. Bass (San Francisco: Jossey-Bass Publishers, 1997).
10. Hans Küng, *Theology for the Third Millennium: An Ecumenical View* (New York: Doubleday, 1988), 209.

Chapter 10

1. Verne Gay, "Is Walter Cronkite the Last Trustworthy Man in America?" *Los Angeles Times Magazine* (January 21, 1996): 10.
2. Ibid., 11.
3. For a further discussion on the relationship of trust to leadership, see Carnegie Samuel Calian, *Where's the Passion for Excellence in the Church?* (Wilton, Conn.: Morehouse Publishing, 1989), 41–44; and Stephen L. Carter, *Integrity* (New York: Basic Books, 1996).
4. John W. Gardner, *Building Community* (Washington, D.C.: Independent Sector, 1991), 17. See also Gardner's book, *On Leadership* (New York: Free Press, 1990) and Jürgen Moltmann, *The Source of Life: The Holy Spirit and the Theology of Life,* (Minneapolis: Fortress Press, 1997), especially pp. 89–102.
5. According to Barna Research Group of Glendale, California, church attendance is presently at its lowest level in two decades. It is reported that 37 percent of Americans now go to church on a given Sunday. Not only is attendance going down, but in a

graying culture we have graying congregations (*The Presbyterian Outlook* [September 30, 1996]: 3. G. Lloyd Rediger's recent work, *Clergy Killers* (Louisville, Ky.: Westminster John Knox Press, 1997), reports that approximately 60 percent of pastors function competently, even effectively, and at least one-fourth have been forced out of one or more congregations and many more are severely stressed and vulnerable. In other words, a pastor is being "fired" (forced out) every six minutes in the United States (pp. 6–7). This is certainly a serious state of affairs that reflects sadly on the church as the people of God (clergy and laity), who ought to be in a more effective and supportive partnership together.

6. Kennon L. Callahan, *Effective Church Leadership* (San Francisco: Harper, 1990), 3, 13, 22.

Afterword

1. Charles Trueheart, "Welcome to the Next Church," *Atlantic Monthly* (August 1996): 38.
2. See Russell L. Ackoff, *Redesigning the Future: A Systems Approach to Societal Problems* (New York: John Wiley & Sons, 1974).
3. See Lyle E. Schaller, *The New Reformation: Tomorrow Arrived Yesterday* (Nashville: Abingdon Press, 1995); Tony Campolo, *Can Mainline Denominations Make a Comeback?* (Valley Forge, Pa.: Judson Press, 1995); George G. Hunter III, *Church for the Unchurched* (Nashville: Abingdon Press, 1996); Milton J. Coalter, John M. Mulder, and Louis B. Weeks, *Vital Signs: The Promises of Mainstream Protestantism* (Grand Rapids: Eerdmans, 1996): Leander E. Keck, *The Church Confident* (Nashville: Abingdon Press, 1993); Letty M. Russell, *The Church in the Round* (Louisville, Ky.: Westminster John Knox Press, 1993); Jürgen Moltmann, *The Church in the Power of the Spirit* (London: SCM Press, 1977); and James H. Evans, *We Have Been Believers* (Minneapolis: Fortress Press, 1992).
4. I wish to express my appreciation to John W. Gardner of Stanford University (formerly secretary of Health, Education, and Welfare for the United States and founder of Common Cause and the Independent Sector) for insightful remarks in our discussion together and for his helpful booklet, *Building Community* (Washington, D.C.: Independent Sector, 1991).

BIBLIOGRAPHY

Anderson, Leith. *A Church for the 21st Century*. Minneapolis: Bethany House, 1992.

Baptism-Eucharist-Ministry. World Council of Churches Publication, 1992.

Berkhof, Hendrikus. *Christian Faith*. Chapters 38–41. Grand Rapids: Wm. B. Eerdmans Publishing Co., 1979.

Boff, Leonardo. *The Church: Charism and Power*. Chapter 7. New York: Crossroad, 1985.

Buchanan, John M. *Being Church, Becoming Community*. Louisville, Ky.: Westminster John Knox Press, 1996.

Calian, Carnegie Samuel. *Theology without Boundaries: Encounters of Eastern Orthodoxy and Western Tradition*. (Louisville, Ky.: Westminster/John Knox Press, 1992.

——. *Where's the Passion for Excellence in the Church?* Wilton, Conn.: Morehouse Publishing, 1989.

Calvin, John. *Institutes of the Christian Religion*. Ed. John J. McNeill. Library of Christian Classics Vol. XX and XXI (Philadelphia: Westminster Press, 1960).

Campolo, Tony. *Can Mainline Denominations Make a Comeback?* Valley Forge, Pa.: Judson Press, 1995.

Carroll, Jackson and Wade Clark Roof, eds. *Beyond Establishment*. Louisville, Ky.: Westminster/John Knox Press, 1993.

Coalter, Milton J., John M. Mulder, and Louis B. Weeks. *Vital Signs: The Promises of Mainstream Protestantism*. Grand Rapids: Eerdmans, 1996.

Cobb Jr., John B. *Reclaiming the Church*. Louisville, Ky.: Westminster John Knox Press, 1997.

Dawn, Marva J. *Reaching Out without Dumbing Down*. Grand Rapids: Wm. B. Eerdmans Publishing Co., 1995.

Dulles, Avery. *Models of the Church*. New York: Image Books, 1987.

Easum, William. *Dancing with Dinosaurs: Ministry in a Hostile and Hurting World*. Nashville: Abingdon Press, 1993.

Foster, Charles R. and Theodore Brelsford. *We Are the Church Together*. Philadelphia: Trinity Press, 1996.

Gerrish, B. A. *Grace and Gratitude: The Eucharistic Theology of John Calvin*. Minneapolis: Fortress Press, 1993.

Hadaway, C. Kirk and David A. Roozen. *Rerouting the Protestant Mainstream*. Nashville: Abingdon Press, 1995.

Haugk, Kenneth C. *Antagonists in the Church*. Minneapolis: Augsburg Publishing House, 1988.

Hawkins, Thomas R. *The Learning Congregation*. Louisville, Ky.: Westminster John Knox Press, 1997.

Hodgson, Peter. *Revisioning the Church*. Minneapolis: Fortress Press, 1988.

Hunter, George. *Church for the Unchurched*. Nashville: Abingdon Press, 1996.

Keck, Leander. *Church Confident*. Nashville: Abingdon Press, 1993.

Küng, Hans. *The Church*. New York: Image Books, 1987.

————. *Credo*. New York: Doubleday, 1993.

Lewis, Harold T. *Yet with a Steady Beat*. Philadelphia: Trinity Press, 1996.

Moltmann, Jürgen. *The Church in the Power of the Spirit*. New York: Harper & Row, 1977.

————. *The Crucified God*. New York: Harper & Row, 1974.

————. *Theology of Hope*. London: SCM Press, 1967.

Moore, Peter C. *A Church to Believe In*. Solon, Ohio: Latimer Press, 1994.

Morris, Linus J. *The High Impact Church*. Houston: Touch Publications, 1993.

Mudge, Lewis S., *The Sense of a People*. Philadelphia: Trinity Press International, 1992.

Mullin, Robert B. and Russell E. Richey, eds. *Reimagining Denominationalism*. Oxford: Oxford University Press, 1994.

Naisbitt, John and Patricia Aburdene. *Megatrends 2000*. New York: Avon Books, 1990.

Olsen, Charles M. *Transforming Church Boards*. Washington, D.C.: Alban Institute, 1995.

Pannenberg, W. *The Church*. Philadelphia: Westminster Press, 1983.

Raiser, Konrad. *To Be the Church*. Geneva: WCC Publications, 1997.

Rediger, G. Lloyd. *Clergy Killers*. Louisville, Ky.: Westminster John Knox Press, 1997.

Reeves, Thomas C. *The Empty Church*. New York: Free Press, 1996.

Roberts, J. D. *The Prophethood of Black Believers: An African-American Political Theology for Ministry*. Louisville, Ky.: Westminster John Knox Press, 1994.

Roof, Wade Clark. *A Generation of Seekers*. San Francisco: Harper, 1993.

Russell, Letty M. *Church in the Round*. Louisville, Ky.: Westminster/John Knox Press, 1993.

Schaller, Lyle E. *The New Reformation*. Nashville: Abingdon Press, 1995.

Schüssler-Fiorenza, Elisabeth. *In Memory of Her*. New York: Crossroad, 1992.

Senge, Peter M. *The Fifth Discipline: The Art and Practice of the Organization.* New York: Doubleday, 1994.

Sittser, Gerald L. *A Grace Disguised.* Grand Rapids: Zondervan Publishing House, 1996.

Small, Joseph D. *God and Ourselves: A Brief Exercise in Reformed Theology.* Louisville, Ky.: Presbyterian Publishing Corporation, 1996.

Stookey, L. H. *Eucharist: Christ's Feast with the Church.* Nashville: Abingdon Press, 1993.

van Wijk-Bos, Johanna W. H. *Reformed and Feminist: A Challenge to the Church.* Louisville, Ky.: Westminster/John Knox Press, 1991.

———. *Reimagining God: The Case for Scriptural Diversity.* Louisville, Ky.: Westminster John Knox Press, 1995.

Wainwright, Geoffrey. *Eucharist and Eschatology.* Oxford: Oxford University Press, 1981.

———. *Doxology: The Praise of God in Worship, Doctrine and Life: A Systematic Theology.* Oxford: Oxford University Press, 1980.

Warren, Rick. *The Purpose Driven Church.* Grand Rapids: Zondervan Publishing House, 1995.

Williamson, Parker T. *Standing Firm.* Philadelphia: PLC Publications, 1996.

Wind, James P. and James W. Lewis, eds. *American Congregations.* Vols. 1 and 2. Chicago: University of Chicago Press, 1994.

INDEX OF NAMES

DATE DUE

Demco, Inc. 38-293